40873690R00057

This book is dedicated to my Heavenly Father Yahweh, His Son Yeshua, and His Holy Spirit that dwells inside of me! Thank you for being my Creator, my Father, my Savior, and my Counselor! Thank you for loving me with your unconditional and majestic love! I give you all the praise and glory!

# COPYRIGHT DISCLAIMER
## Copyright 2022 by Judy Jacobson

# WELCOME

A little bit about myself...

I was born and raised in St. Louis Missouri. I grew up in a loving, middle-class, Christian home. After graduating college with a Chemical Engineering degree, I spent the next 12 years in the business world. During this time, I met and married my husband, Steve Jacobson.

After our third son was born, I was blessed to be a stay-at-home mom for our three active boys, which became my second career for the next 12 years.

Then in 2011, Yahweh suddenly called me to my third career to write, pray, and teach for his Kingdom purposes. My new "dream" job is full of adventure, excitement and fulfillment, and is something I know I will do for the rest of my life. My passionate mission in life is to teach Christians the HOW TO's of walking in Jesus's footsteps, by forming an intimate relationship with Yahweh and Jesus, through the Holy Spirit that dwells inside of them. My husband and I, and our adult children, currently live in Georgia.

*Love, Judy Jacobson*

AUTHOR   EDUCATOR   SPEAKER

# God 99
## *I want everything*

Life as I knew it changed on the night I raised my hands in the air and said, "God, I want **EVERYTHING** the Holy Spirit has to offer me! Don't hold back!" I made this request with no agenda in mind. For the first time ever, I truly surrendered my entire life to Yahweh's will.

From that day forward **EVERYTHING** changed. Quickly, I came to find out that the Holy Spirit has a lot to offer. Over the next several years, Yahweh asked me to write a book about his divine name, start a prophetic prayer ministry, lay hands on the sick, and teach Christians how to hear his majestic voice.

What immediately changed, after that night, was my ability to hear Yahweh's precious voice through his Holy Spirit. Suddenly, his voice became very loud and very clear to me, in an abundance of ways. By hearing Yahweh's voice day after day after day, my mind and thoughts became transformed and renewed with **HIS TRUTH**, and my soul was set free from all of Satan's oppressions.

Quickly, I became totally submerged in Yahweh's **LIVING WATERS**, and started experiencing unexplainable peace, love, and joy. Over the years, my favorite place to hang out became my Heavenly Father's **PRESENCE**. To this day, I still cannot get enough of **HIM** or his majestic voice.

I have been on this glorious journey of discovery for 12 years now. During my journey, Yahweh has given me many **KEYS** to the **KINGDOM** that have set me on a life of freedom and abundant living.

I wrote this short, yet power packed, book in order to share just a few highlights of what I have learned, so that you too can benefit from these **KEYS**. I pray, after spending time in Yahweh's Presence that your **FATHER'S HOUSE** becomes your favorite place to hang out as well. I pray that you too become addicted to his powerful and loving voice, and that your life is set ablaze with his glory!

*Love, Judy Jacobson*

# 12 Keys to FREEDOM and the *Abundant Life*

01 Key- Start a Holy Brainwashing Routine

02 Key- Engage with the Holy Spirit Daily

03 Key- Discover Yahweh's Majestic Voice

04 Key- Pray, Listen, and Journal

05 Key- Receive Deliverance for your Soul

06 Key- Know Thy Enemy Satan

07 Key- Stop Aiding and Abetting the Enemy

08 Key- Pick up your Sword of the Spirit

09 Key- Receive the Baptism of the Holy Spirit

10 Key- Discover your Gifts of the Holy Spirit

11 Key- Utilize the Gift of Speaking in Tongues

12 Key- Engage with Yahweh's Angels

# Here is my personal advice for ALL believers in Jesus Christ:

These **12 KEYS** are essential for all Christians. I give these keys to everyone I meet, because after I became a believer in Jesus Christ, even though I immediately started attending Bible study and church weekly, I was still what I would consider a baby Christian even after 12 years of doing so.

Even though I definitely knew what the Bible said **ABOUT** Yahweh and Jesus, I didn't **KNOW** Yahweh and Jesus. There is a huge difference in having knowledge about someone, and knowing them. As a result, I did not have an intimate relationship with my Heavenly Father.

In addition, I had little knowledge about the Holy Spirit, his role in allowing me to hear Yahweh and Jesus's personal voice, or the spiritual gifts he had to offer. I had never heard of the Baptism of the Holy Spirit, and I didn't know anything about the powerful gift of speaking in tongues.

In all of my Bible studies, I was never taught about Satan, his kingdom, or the power and authority I have over him in Christ Jesus. I had no idea that my soul needed deliverance. And no one had every told me that the Word of God is my defensive weapon against my enemy, that I have to pick up and verbally speak out loud in order to be effective.

Finally, I knew there were angels in Yahweh's kingdom, but I sure didn't know their role was to help me in my walk with Jesus, and that I needed to utilize them often.

It was only after 12 years of thoroughly studying the Bible that I knew that there was something missing in my walk with Jesus. So I asked Yahweh, **"IS THIS IT? IS THIS ALL THERE IS? THERE MUST BE MORE!"**

**WOW**...What Yahweh revealed to me is, **"YES...THERE IS MORE...MUCH MORE!!!"** What follows are the **"HIGHLIGHTS of the MORE"** that Yahweh desires for all of his children, in order to create a richer, abundant, and deeper life with him!

# Key #1 Start a Holy Brainwashing Routine

*"It was for Freedom that Christ set us Free"*

On the day of your salvation, Yahweh's Holy Spirit comes to dwell inside of you. It is on this day that your spirit is made brand new. The spirit of the world is pushed out, and replaced with Yahweh's Holy Spirit. This is the dynamic that Paul was talking about when he said, "Therefore, if anyone is in Christ, he is a new creation; the old is gone, the new has come!" (2 Corinthians 5:17)

Becoming a brand-new creation sounds incredibly awesome … which it is! Except what most believers do not understand is that a person's being consists of a **SPIRIT**, a **SOUL** and a **BODY**. So, it is true that your **SPIRIT** is made completely brand new on the day of your salvation. However, what most people don't know is that our **SOUL**, which consists of your mind, your will, and your emotions, does not change one iota.

Since your soul controls your body, your thoughts, your beliefs, your actions, and the words that come out of your mouth, unless you receive complete healing and deliverance of all your past and current traumas, sins, worldly habits, addictions, and false beliefs, on the same day as your salvation, you will have some work to do moving forward in order to experience the abundant living that Jesus promises believers. (John 10:10)

Therefore, it becomes extremely important, after you become a believer in Jesus Christ, to start what I call a **HOLY BRAINWASHING ROUTINE**. This routine consists of reading your Bible on a daily basis, spending quality time in Yahweh's Presence, praying, worshipping, listening for his majestic voice, and listening to Christian music in your car and home.

The purpose of this daily Holy Brainwashing Routine is so that you can put off your **OLD WORLDLY IDENTITY**, and put on your **NEW IDENTITY IN JESUS CHRIST**, as a son or daughter of Yahweh. If you are consistent with this routine of engaging with Yahweh daily, you will successfully exchange your mind, your will, and your emotions for the mind of Jesus Christ, the will of Yahweh, and heavenly emotions. Your worldly thoughts, desires, sinful ways, and habits will be exchanged for godly truth, and as a result your new life with your Savior Jesus will be filled with **PEACE**, **LOVE**, **JOY** and a **SOUND MIND**.

Heaven on earth will be your new physical reality, because your **SOUL WILL REFLECT** Yahweh's Holy Spirit inside of you! For when your soul is renewed, your body is sure to follow. **WOW** … sounds like abundant living at its finest!

www.JUDYJACOBSONMINISTRIES.com

# Key 1

*Freedom*

**John 10:10**
"The thief comes only to kill, steal, and destroy; I (Jesus) came that they may have **LIFE**, and have it **ABUNDANTLY**."

**Romans 12:1-2**
I appeal to you therefore, brethren, by the mercies of God, to present your bodies as a **LIVING SACRIFICE**, holy and acceptable to God, which is your spiritual worship. Do not be conformed to this world but be transformed by the **RENEWAL OF YOUR MIND**, that you may prove what is the will of God, what is good and acceptable and perfect.

**1 Thessalonians 5:23 (ESV)**
May the God of peace himself **SANCTIFY YOU COMPLETELY**; and may your whole **SPIRIT** and **SOUL** and **BODY** be kept blameless at the coming of our Lord Jesus Christ.

**2 Timothy 2:21 (ESV)**
Therefore, if anyone **CLEANSES** himself from what is dishonorable, he will be a vessel for honorable use, **SET APART AS HOLY**, useful to the master of the house, ready for every good work.

**John 8:31-32**
"If you **CONTINUE IN MY WORD**, you are truly my disciples, and you will **KNOW THE TRUTH**, and **THE TRUTH WILL SET YOU FREE**."

**1 Chronicles 16:23-31 (ESV)**
**SING TO YAHWEH**, all the earth; **PROCLAIM** his salvation day after day. **DECLARE** his glory among the nations, his marvelous deeds among all peoples. For great is Yahweh and most worthy of praise; he is to be feared above all gods. For all the gods of the nations are idols, but Yahweh made the heavens. Splendor and majesty are before him; strength and joy are in his dwelling place. Ascribe to Yahweh, all you families of nations, ascribe to Yahweh glory and strength. **ASCRIBE** to Yahweh the glory due his name; bring an offering and come before him. **WORSHIP** Yahweh in the splendor of his holiness. **TREMBLE** before him, all the earth! The world is firmly established; it cannot be moved. Let the heavens rejoice, let the earth be glad; let them **SAY** among the nations, "**YAHWEH REIGNS**!"

**Joshua 1:8**
This book of the law shall not depart out of your mouth, but you shall **MEDITATE ON IT** day and night, that you are careful to do according to all that is written in it; for then you shall make your way prosperous, and then you shall have good success.

## KEY #1 QUESTIONS:

In order to create a healthy habit of meeting daily with your Heavenly Father, you first need to decide on **WHEN** and **WHERE** is the best time and place to meet with him. Therefore, ask your Heavenly Father these questions and expect him to reply:

Father, **WHEN** do you want to meet with me, as only you know the best time for me to focus on our relationship...morning, before I go to work, lunchtime, evening?

_____

_____

_____

Father, **WHERE** do you want to meet me...in my prayer closet, sitting on my favorite chair, in my car, while I'm working out? Where is **OUR SPOT** where you want to meet me daily?

_____

_____

_____

Father, **WHAT** book of the Bible do you want me to read first, as I start my Holy Brainwashing Routine? And, should I read the Bible or listen to it audibly through a Bible app?

_____

_____

_____

Experts will tell you it takes 21 days to create a new habit, therefore I challenge you to meet with your Heavenly Father for the next 21 days at the time and place that Yahweh designates. Then see what miraculous things take place in your time together. Take notice of the benefits of committing to creating your new habit. Ask Yahweh's Holy Spirit to speak to you daily, leading you on when and what to read, when to pray, when to listen, when to worship. Remember, Yahweh is your loving Father, Creator, and Savior. Therefore, when you enter into his Presence daily, know with certainty that HE is so excited you have decided to spend your valuable time with him!

**PRAYER:** Heavenly Father, as your precious child, I look forward to meeting with you, sensing your Holy Presence and feeling your heavenly embrace. During our times together, I pray that you will fully awaken my spiritual senses to your **PRESENCE** and to your **VOICE**. I ask for you to open my **EYES** to see you in ways they have never seen you before. I ask you to open my **EARS** to hear your personal words for me. I ask you to open my **HEART** to feel your unconditional love for me. I ask you to open my **MIND** to fully understand the truth and mysteries of **YOU**, **JESUS**, the **HOLY SPIRIT**, and your **LIVING WORD**. Finally, I ask for you to encounter me in ways I have never encountered you before, and prove to me that my inheritance on earth is **FREEDOM** and **ABUNDANT LIVING**! I pray all of these things in the mighty name of your beloved Son, Jesus Christ of Nazareth. Amen!

# Father, What else do you want me to know, understand, or believe?

# Key #2 Engage with the Holy Spirit Daily

One morning I woke up to Yahweh saying, "For it is one thing to **QUENCH** the Holy Spirit, and yet another to **GRIEVE** the Holy Spirit. But it is entirely different when one **BLASPHEMY'S** or speaks against the Holy Spirit. **THESE ARE MY RULES OF ENGAGEMENT!**"

On the day we put our faith in Jesus Christ as our Lord and Savior, we are given a deposit of the Holy Spirit within us. On this day scripture says that our Heavenly Father Yahweh deposits his Spirit in Jesus's holy name into our hearts (John 14:26).

On this day we are sealed with the Holy Spirit as a guarantee of our inheritance until the day we acquire possession of it (2 Corinthians 1:21-22, Ephesians 1:13-14).

The deposit of the Holy Spirit within us is like our engagement ring, until our wedding day takes place. Our wedding day occurs at Jesus's second coming when he raptures us into heaven and we are invited to the marriage supper of the Lamb (Revelation 19:9). Until then, for all who believe in Jesus Christ, an engagement ring is given as a pledge or a promise from God that he will always be faithful to us. And if we are faithful in return, and **DO NOT** call off the engagement by turning away from Jesus, the wedding is sure to follow. Until our wedding day occurs, Scripture says that the Bride is to make herself ready (Revelation 19:7).

So, how do we prepare ourselves for Jesus's return and our wedding day? According to Yahweh's personal word to me, and according to Scripture, we do so by engaging daily with the Holy Spirit within us, being careful not to grieve, to quench, or to blasphemy the Holy Spirit, so that we can **INTIMATELY** get to know our bridegroom Jesus, and our Heavenly Father Yahweh.

If you follow these three important **RULES OF ENGAGEMENT**, you are sure to live an abundant life on planet earth, and you will be prepared and ready to meet your bridegroom on your wedding day. You will have become **ONE** with Yahweh and Jesus through their Holy Spirit within you.

So, what does it mean to not grieve, quench, or blasphemy the Holy Spirit? In order to fully understand these commandments, we must first look at the role of the Holy Spirit in a believer's life, according to Jesus.

      www.JUDYJACOBSONMINISTRIES.com

# Key 2

## Engage

"If you love me, you will keep my commandments. And I will pray the Father, and he will give you another Counselor, to be with you for ever, even the **SPIRIT OF TRUTH**, whom the world cannot receive, because it neither sees him nor knows him; you know him, for he **DWELLS WITH YOU,** and **WILL BE IN YOU.**" (John 14:15-17)

"These things I have spoken to you, while I am still with you. But the **COUNSELOR**, the Holy Spirit, whom the Father will send in my name, he will **TEACH YOU** all things, and bring to your remembrance all that I have said to you. **PEACE I LEAVE WITH YOU; MY PEACE I GIVE TO YOU**; not as the world gives do I give to you." (John 14:25-27)

"Nevertheless, I tell you the truth: it is to **YOUR ADVANTAGE** that I go away, for if I do not go away, **THE COUNSELOR** will not come to you; but if I go, **I WILL SEND HIM TO YOU**...I have many things to say to you, but you cannot bear them now. When the Spirit of truth comes, he will **GUIDE YOU** into all the truth; for he will not speak on his own authority, but **WHATEVER HE HEARS HE WILL SPEAK,** and he will **DECLARE TO YOU** the things that are to come. He will glorify me, for he will take what is mine and **DECLARE IT TO YOU**. All that the Father has is mine; therefore I said that he will take what is mine and **DECLARE IT TO YOU**." (John 16:7,12-15)

According to Scripture, the Holy Spirit dwells inside of a believer, and is the direct communication link between the believer and their Heavenly Father Yahweh and their Savior Jesus. Whatever the Holy Spirit hears Yahweh or Jesus speak in heaven, he will **DECLARE** it to you. He is described as a believer's **COUNSELOR** and **TEACHER**. Jesus describes the Holy Spirit as **HIS PEACE**. The Holy Spirit's role is to **GUIDE** the believer into **ALL TRUTH** in order to set them completely free from the sins of the world, and Satan's lies.

Jesus declared that the Holy Spirit is given to us for our **ADVANTAGE**. The word advantage means, "a condition or circumstance that puts one in a favorable or superior position." Therefore, Jesus is telling us that by having the Holy Spirit dwelling inside of us, believers will have a favorable and superior position in life, because Jesus will be with us at all times.

From this knowledge of the Holy Spirit's role in a believer's life, we can easily see why we are to be careful not to grieve, quench, or blasphemy the Holy Spirit within us. We are given the Holy Spirit for our benefit. It is Yahweh's ultimate gift to us for abundant living. For when we **LISTEN** to and then **OBEY** what the Holy Spirit is declaring to us, we will inevitably have more favorable outcomes and greater opportunities for success in every area of our lives.

Also, since the Holy Spirit is **LIFE ITSELF**, when you engage with the Holy Spirit daily, Scripture tells us that you will produce the **FRUITS** of Yahweh's Holy Spirit, which are peace, love, joy, goodness, kindness, gentleness, patience, faithfulness, and self-control (Galatians 5:22-23). Finally, by engaging with the Holy Spirit daily and listening for Yahweh's majestic voice, you are inviting **LIFE** and **LIGHT** into all of your circumstances.

The word engage means, **"to participate or become involved in."**

The word grieve means, **"to cause great sorrow, sadness, or a deep ache."**

The word quench means, **"to extinguish or put out the fire or light."**

The word blasphemy means, **"to speak against, or show great disrespect to something holy."**

Therefore, in a nutshell, believers grieve and quench the Holy Spirit when they **KNOWINGLY** or **UNKNOWINGLY** chose to participate or become involved in anything of Satan or the evil spirits of his world. We cause the Holy Spirit great sorrow and extinquish his fire within us, when we close our eyes to his light and truth and instead chose to continue living by the ways of the world, which bring death and darkness.

For the **FRUITS OF SATAN'S WORLD** are warfare, hatred, misery, cruelty, hostility, roughness, impatience, disloyalty, instability, worry, sickness, depression, anxiety, unforgiveness, bitterness, anger, sin, addictions, failed marriages, ruined relationships, oppression, the list goes on and on.

You can easily tell if you are grieving or quenching the Holy Spirit if any of the fruits of Satan's world are apparent in your life. What it means is you are in some way engaging with Satan's ways or his demonic spirits, which is causing the Holy Spirit great sorrow and sadness.

Since there are countless ways in which we can grieve and quench the Holy Spirit, it is extremely important to ask Yahweh himself, "Father, how am I grieving and quenching your precious Holy Spirit within me?" For only he can tell you, so expect to hear a reply. Since Yahweh desires for you to experience an abundant life, he will tell you exactly how and in what area you are **HINDERING** the work of the Holy Spirit within you.

When you become aware of the ways in which you are grieving and quenching the Holy Spirit, you can then ask Yahweh to help you change your ways. By doing so you will no longer be stopping the flow of his **LIVING WATERS** through you, and instead you will experience the fruits of Yahweh's heavenly peace, love and joy manifesting in your heart, and in every area of your life.

Both quenching and grieving the Holy Spirit are similar in their effects. Both hinder a godly lifestyle. Both happen when a believer sins against Yahweh and follows his or her own worldly desires. The only correct road to follow is the road that leads the believer closer to Yahweh and purity, and farther away from the world and sin, so that nothing will stand in your way of intimately getting to know your Heavenly Father, Yahweh, and your Bridegroom, Jesus. Just as we do not like to be grieved, and just as we do not seek to quench what is good—so we should not grieve or quench the Holy Spirit by refusing to follow his lead.

Finally, when you blasphemy the Holy Spirit, it shows you do not **VALUE** what Jesus did on the cross on your behalf. When you speak against and disrespect the Holy Spirit, you are ultimately telling Yahweh that Jesus's **SACRIFICE** of his **LIFE**, so that you could have eternal life through his gift of the Holy Spirit, was **NOT ENOUGH**! That is why blaspheming the Holy Spirit is an unforgivable sin.

For when you blasphemy the Holy Spirit, you are blaspheming **LIFE ITSELF!**

**Ephesians 4:30**

"**AND DO NOT GRIEVE THE HOLY SPIRIT OF GOD**, by whom you were sealed for the day of redemption."

**1 Thessalonians 5:19-20**

"**DO NOT QUENCH THE SPIRIT**, do not despise prophesying, but test everything; hold fast what is good, abstain from every form of evil."

**Matthew 12:31-32**

"Therefore I tell you, every sin and blasphemy will be forgiven men, but the **BLASPHEMY AGAINST THE SPIRIT WILL NOT BE FORGIVEN**. And whoever says a word against the Son of man will be forgiven; but whoever **SPEAKS AGAINST THE HOLY SPIRIT** will not be forgiven, either in this age or in the age to come.

**Psalm 103:1-5**

Bless Yahweh, O my soul; and all that is within me, **BLESS HIS HOLY NAME**!

Bless Yahweh, O my soul, and **FORGET NOT ALL HIS BENEFITS**,

who **FORGIVES** all your iniquity,

who **HEALS** all your diseases,

who **REDEEMS** your life from the Pit,

who **CROWNS** you with steadfast love and mercy,

who **SATISFIES** you with good as long as you live

so that your youth is **RENEWED** like the eagle's.

**KEY #2 QUESTIONS:**
Look back at the definitions of "grieve" and "quench," and then ask Yahweh these questions, while considering every aspect of your life:

Father, in what ways am I currently **GRIEVING** your Holy Spirit within me?

_____

_____

_____

_____

_____

Father, how am I currently **QUENCHING** the works of your Holy Spirit within me?

_____

_____

_____

_____

_____

Father, right now, please show me specific ways in which I can intentionally **ENGAGE** with your Holy Spirit throughout my day?

_____

_____

_____

_____

_____

_____

_____

**PRAYER:** Heavenly Father, thank you for your rules of engagement! I now understand your rules are **KEYS** to life itself. For when we grieve, quench, and blasphemy the Holy Spirit, we are hindering your **LIVING WATERS** from flowing through us and from experiencing abundance. Thank you Father, for sending your Son Jesus to die for my sins, so that I could receive the most precious gift of your Holy Spirit dwelling inside of me. I now understand he is my Counselor, Teacher, and Spirit of Truth. Please forgive me for all of the times I have knowingly or unknowingly grieved and quenched the Holy Spirit within me. From this day forward, I give you permission to make me acutely aware of the ways in which I am hindering the Holy Spirit's work in my life, so I can first repent and then make the needed changes. Please show me the life transformation that takes place when I choose to engage with your Holy Spirit daily, in every decision, every thought, every action, and every word that comes out of my mouth. I ask you all of these things in Jesus's precious name. Amen!

# Father, What else do you want me to know, understand, or believe?

# Key #3 Discover Yahweh's Majestic Voice

I remember the first day I encountered Yahweh like it was yesterday. It happened the day after I **PLEADED** with Yahweh to give me a personal sign: first that he existed, and second that he cared about me and my family. Wow...not only did he give me a **HUGE SIGN** on that day, which proved to me that he exists, but he also convinced me of just how deeply he loves me and my family. The details of this encounter are recorded in my book titled, **"Encountering the Great I AM: With His Name Comes Everything!"**

On this day Yahweh **SPOKE** very loudly to me in my spirit, as he was simultaneously **SHOWING** me something only my Heavenly Father could show me. As I was physically looking at the remains of what had been a raging fire in my clothes dryer, which consisted of black ashes and deformed metal, Yahweh said very loudly to me, **"This is life without me, perfectly white on the outside, black and charred remains on the inside."** Oh my ... his words hit me **DEEP** in my heart!

As soon as I **HEARD** Yahweh's voice speak to me so clearly, I knew without a doubt that he existed. I was sure of his existence, because what Yahweh was showing me on that day was the **CONDITION** of my **HEART**. For only my Heavenly Father, my Lord, and my Savior knew that my heart was broken in a million pieces, which was exactly what the ashes and charred remains in my dryer represented. On that day, Yahweh told me to give him my heart, so he could mend my broken heart and make it brand new. I obeyed!

From that day forward, my relationship with Yahweh changed, all because I actually heard Yahweh's personal words for me and me alone. His voice convinced me that he is the all-knowing, powerful and loving Creator, and Savior of this world that I could safely commit my life to. He also convinced me that **EVERYTHING** I read in the Bible is absolute truth, and only he can show me the **DEEP** and **HIDDEN** things in my life that need attention. Quickly after that day, I gave my life to Jesus, Yahweh's Holy Spirit came to dwell inside of me, and I started my new life as a daughter of the **LIVING GOD**.

It would take another 12 years before I started hearing Yahweh's voice daily, through all of the ways in which he speaks, because at that point in my journey all I knew to do is go to Church and to Bible Study. For it would take another powerful encounter, this time with Yahweh's Holy Spirit, before I discovered Yahweh desires to personally **SPEAK** to his children daily through his Holy Spirit that dwells within us.

What I want to share with you is Yahweh's personal words he gave me on August 29, 2016 about his **MAJESTIC VOICE** and all it can accomplish in a believer's life. **ENJOY**!

www.JUDYJACOBSONMINISTRIES.com

# Yahweh's Majestic Voice

## (God's words spoken to Judy Jacobson 8/29/2016)

My Prayer: Father, I believe that since you created the universe and everything in it that you can speak to me, your creation, in a multitude of ways. I believe your words in scripture that promise that you will speak to me through the Holy Spirit. Jesus said, "**My sheep hear my voice**, and I know them, and they follow me" John 10:27. Sometimes we read verses so often that we gloss over their actual meaning. Jesus said my sheep "**HEAR**" my voice. What that means is that Jesus "**SPEAKS**" to his children. It means that his voice can be heard. In Revelation 3:20 Jesus says, "Behold, I stand at the door and knock. **If anyone HEARS my voice AND OPENS THE DOOR**, I will come in to him and eat with him, and he with me." Once we believe that Jesus wants to actually speak to us, and we open the door to HIS voice, he will come and commune with us regularly.

Question: Father, what do you want me to know about your voice?
(The bolded words are the words God's said to me. The other words are my own interpretation.)

**It's like a flower**: It starts as a seed, grows roots, bursts through the soil, forms a stem and leaves, and finally develops into a beautiful flower. After the flower dies, growth continues as seeds grow in the flower head that eventually drop into other people's lives.
**It's beautiful**
**It's majestic...like my name**
"The voice of Yahweh is majestic." Psalm 29:4
"O Yahweh, our Lord, how majestic is thy name in all the earth." Psalm 8:1
**It has a purpose**
**It frees**
**It liberates**
**It unbinds**
**It instructs and guides**
**It awakens ME** (the Holy Spirit) **within you**
**It loosens strongholds**
**It strengthens the weak**
**It enables victory**
**My written Word is truth**
**My voice ELECTRIFIES my written Word.**
**TOGETHER they EMPOWER you**
**My voice makes Scripture PERSONAL**
**My voice raises the dead to life**
**It provokes wisdom**
**It brings a death to yourself** (old self)
**It renews your mind**

Question: What else do you want me to know about your voice?

**Henry**

Meaning of the name Henry in "The Name Book"

**Ruler of the Household, Trusted**, Psalm 37:23, **"The steps of a good man are ordered by Yahweh, and he delights in his way."**

Yahweh's voice should be the ruler of your household, and can be trusted!

**Yes, I speak through names**

**From the beginning**

Question: Is there anything else Father you want me to know?

**My voice and Scripture go HAND IN HAND!**

# Bible Verses:

**Psalm 29:3-9**
**The voice of Yahweh rolls over the water.**
The God of glory thunders.
Yahweh shouts over raging water.
**The voice of Yahweh is powerful.**
**The voice of Yahweh is majestic**
**The voice of Yahweh breaks the cedars.**
Yahweh splinter the cedars of Lebanon.
He makes Lebanon skip along like a calf and Mount Sirion like a wild ox.
**The voice of Yahweh strikes with flashes of lightning.**
**The voice of Yahweh makes the wilderness tremble.**
Yahweh splits the oaks and strips the trees of the forests bare. Everyone in his temple is saying, "Glory!"

**Isaiah 30:21**
"and when you turn to the right hand, and when you turn to the left, your ears **will hear a voice behind you, saying, 'This is the way. Walk in it.'"**

**Jeremiah 33:2-3**
"Thus says the LORD who made the earth, the LORD who formed it to establish it—Yahweh is his name: Call to me and **I will answer you, and will tell you** great and hidden things which you have not known."

**John 10:27**
"**My sheep hear my voice**, and I know them, and they follow me."

**John 16:13-15**
"When the Spirit of truth (Holy Spirit) comes, he will guide you into all the truth; for he will not speak on his own authority, but whatever he hears he will speak, and **he will declare to you** the things that are to come. He will glorify me, for he will take what is mine and **declare it to you**. All that the Father has is mine; therefore I said that he will take what is mine and **declare it to you**."

**Revelation 3:20**
"Behold, I stand at the door and knock. **If anyone hears MY VOICE AND OPENS THE DOOR**, I will come in to him and eat with him, and he with me."

**KEY #3 QUESTIONS:**
Go back down through memory lane, and describe in detail your very first encounter with Yahweh or Jesus. Journal what he said to you on that day?

_____

_____

_____

What did Yahweh's message to you accomplish in that moment?

_____

_____

_____

How did Yahweh's voice impact your life from that day forward?

_____

_____

_____

As excited as you were when you encountered your Heavenly Father, Lord, and Savior, Yahweh was equally excited to encounter you, knowing that it would start your relationship with him. Ask Yahweh to reveal to you how excited he was to encounter you on that specific day. Ask him, right now, what that day meant to him and then record it here.

_____

_____

_____

**PRAYER:** Heavenly Father, thank you for unconditionally loving me. Thank you for introducing your Son, Jesus to me. Thank you for sending your Holy Spirit to dwell inside of me, so that I can hear your voice and feel your Presence. Heavenly Father, I desire to hear your voice loudly and frequently, as I am now aware that you want to talk to me. Speak to me daily and I promise to listen and then obey. Show me the power of your majestic voice to liberate, unbind and free me from all the schemes of the enemy. I look forward to experiencing the renewal of my mind and the death to my old self. I look forward to putting on my new Identity in Jesus Christ, as you make me aware of **WHO I AM** to you. I thank you for all of your wisdom and truth that you are going to share with me, so that I can be completely transformed to live with purpose doing your will on earth, as it is in heaven, for the rest of my days. In Jesus's beautiful name, I pray these things. Amen!

# Father, What else do you want me to know, understand, or believe?

The Old Testament is filled with stories of men and women hearing Yahweh's voice. Adam, Noah, Abraham, Isaac, Jacob, Mary, Joseph, Moses, Joshua, King David, Daniel, and all the prophets and prophetesses heard God speak on a regular basis, if not daily. All of these men and women led extraordinary lives, not because they were extraordinary men and women, but because of the extraordinary voice that was guiding and instructing them. These individuals heard Yahweh's voice often either directly from him, through dreams, visions, prophets, or angels of the Lord. And because they were obedient to what they heard, Christians today are still studying these men and women's lives thousands of years later.

Unfortunately, many Christians today do not hear Yahweh's sweet voice, even though they have his Holy Spirit living inside of them, because no one has taught them how. In all of my years of attending church, not once do I remember hearing a sermon preached on how God's children hear his precious voice. Not once were the various methods of hearing and seeing Yahweh's voice taught to me through a preacher or a Sunday school teacher. Oh I learned how to pray, but I was never taught how to hear Yahweh's voice. There is a distinct difference.

Prayer is a powerful way for believers to speak to Yahweh, to allow their voices to be heard. But even if you pray every day that doesn't mean you know how to listen for **HIS REPLY** to your prayers. Since the ways in which Yahweh speaks are not being taught in the churches, that is why I believe most Christians don't hear their Heavenly Father's voice. When someone is unaware something is even possible, why would that individual ever expect to receive it. And since most Christians are not expecting to hear Yahweh's voice daily, his personal words for them go unheard.

You see it is Yahweh's voice that gives you life and makes you extraordinary. If you are not hearing his voice, then you need to start investigating his various ways of communication. From this day forward, make sure to never limit his voice or how he is capable of getting a message to you. And please don't make the mistake of placing Yahweh's voice into the box of Sunday mornings at church. The same ways God communicated with the characters of the Bible is the same way he communicates with believers today. Finally, always remember, "There are no coincidences." If you remember these things and you start searching out his voice daily, you can be sure that your relationship with your Heavenly Father will come alive and your life will be completely transformed.

So, what can you do today to start your own relationship and daily communication with your Heavenly Father? It all comes down to how you position yourself. You need to regularly step out of the chaos of the physical world and into Yahweh's spiritual world so that you can hear his majestic voice.

# Here are some ideas:

- Read your Bible daily, knowing that Yahweh wants to speak directly to you through the words you are reading.

- Go to church in order to hear Yahweh's voice spoken through your pastor.

- Join bible studies and small groups in order to study his Word with others.

- Pray daily. Then intentionally listen for Yahweh's reply. (Prov. 20:12; Jer. 33:2-3; John 10:27; John 16:13-15)

- Pay attention to your dreams. (Joel 2:28; Job 33:15; Acts 2:17)

- Know that Jesus still appears to people in visions. (Joel 2:28; Job 33:15; Acts 2:17)

- Ask Yahweh's Holy Spirit to help you interpret your dreams and visions for meaning.

- Become aware that names and numbers and colors carry biblical significance, and that Yahweh often speaks through them.

- Spend quality time being silent in Yahweh's Presence with no agenda in mind, and ask him, "Father, what is on your heart for me today?"

- While doing so, take notice of the words, thoughts, or phrases that come into your mind that you know are not your own. (1 Corin. 12:8)

- When Yahweh gives you just one word, first look up its definition, and then go to BibleGateway and search every verse in the Bible that has that word in it, in order to discover what he wants you to know.

☐ Analyze the words that complete strangers, possibly angels, speak into your life as perhaps being direct words from God. (Heb. 13:2)

☐ Intentionally look for Yahweh's personal messages through his creation and things that surround you. (Rom. 1:20)

☐ Remember, there are no coincidences.

☐ Pay attention to the lyrics of a song Yahweh places on your lips.

☐ Know that Yahweh may choose to speak to you through friends and family.

☐ Understand that God still uses his children to speak prophecy into other people's lives. (Joel 2:28; Acts 2:17; 1 Corin. 12:10, 14:1,5,39)

☐ Be bold and ask other people who hear Yahweh's voice to teach you how to recognize and find it.

☐ Surround yourself with other believers who are seeking his voice as well.

☐ Ask Yahweh for a full spectrum awakening of all of your spiritual senses to his voice.

☐ Read books on discerning the voice of God.

☐ Start each day with questions such as: Father, what do you want me to know today? What is your will for me today? What does love demand of me today? Who do you say that I am? Who would you like me to pray for today? How can I help you bring heaven to earth? What is your heavenly prescription for me? Expect a reply before the day is over.

☐ Finally, when you do hear Yahweh's voice in a new way and it fills your heart to overflowing, rejoice with your Heavenly Father.

# Key 4 — Listen

Let the mystery of Yahweh's voice be the deep and hidden treasure that you seek, search, and cry out for. If you seek out his voice, you will find it. That is guaranteed! But remember the word **SEEK** is an action word. You must intentionally search for Yahweh's voice, in order to show him your interest in hearing him, before he will respond. But respond he will, because there is nothing that makes Yahweh happier than his children searching for an intimate and personal relationship with him. So be expectant to hear Yahweh's voice. Understand what is possible, and then strategically position yourself, both physically and spiritually, in order to make it happen.

And finally, when you start hearing Yahweh's majestic voice, know that it will begin transforming you from the **ORDINARY to the EXTRAORDINARY**. Make sure that you **RECORD in a JOURNAL** all that Yahweh tells you over the years, so that you too will have proof that you serve a Living God who still speaks to and encounters his children. Once you hear Yahweh's voice regularly, never forget that you too may be commanded to speak to other believers the words he places in your mouth or the visions he places in your sight. Like the men, women, and prophets of old, the words Yahweh gives you may not be for you alone. His words may, in fact, be meant to save the eternal life of another. They may be meant for the person sitting right next to you. Never fail to speak Yahweh's wisdom just because you are afraid of how other people will receive his words. Just like the prophets of old, you need to be ready to speak when Yahweh commands you to, regardless of if his words fall on deaf ears.

To help you interpret your dreams and visions from Yahweh, I highly recommend purchasing the following resources: "**The Name Book**," by Dorothy Astoria; "**Biblical Mathematics: Keys to Scripture Numerics**," by Dr. Ed F. Vallowe; "**The Divinity Code to Understanding your Dreams and Visions**," by Adam F. Thompson and Adrian Beale.

**Matthew 4:4**
"It is written, 'Man shall not **LIVE** by bread alone, but by **EVERY WORD** that proceeds from the **MOUTH OF GOD**.'"

**Proverbs 20:12**
The **HEARING EAR** and the **SEEING EYE**, Yahweh has made them both.

**Jeremiah 30:1-3**
The word that came from Yahweh: "Thus says Yahweh, the God of Israel: **WRITE in a book ALL THE WORDS** that I have spoken to you."

**Habakkuk 2:2**
And Yahweh answered me: "**WRITE THE VISION**; make it plain on tablets, so he may run who reads it."

**KEY #4 QUESTIONS:**
How do you think your life would change if you frequently heard Yahweh's voice?

_____

_____

_____

In what ways have you "heard or seen" Yahweh's voice?

_____

_____

_____

In what ways would you like to hear or see him?

_____

_____

_____

Father, what are the benefits of journaling your personal words, dreams and visions for my life?

_____

_____

_____

I have been journaling everything Yahweh has spoken or showed me since 2011. Because of my obedience of recording every message, he is able to frequently refer me back to his words, dreams and/or visions that he had given me from years prior. Since my journals are in digital form, Yahweh's messages from years past are extremely easy to find. I simply enter in the search bar a key word, and inevitably I am able to locate his message fast. He refers me back often, to the words, dreams or visions that he gave me years prior, because he wants to remind me of what is about to take place, or is already coming to fruition. Yahweh does this in order to prove to me that his personal words are true and can be trusted.

**PRAYER:** Heavenly Father, thank you for your majestic voice. The ways in which you speak to your children are uncountable. Thank you for desiring to speak to me through these multiple ways. Thank you for speaking through dreams and visions and words of knowledge. Thank you for sending your angels to your children with messages. Thank you for speaking to me through your beautiful **WORDS** written in the Bible, and through prophets, pastors, friends, family and strangers. Please encounter me, Father, in all of your boundless ways of communication. Again I ask for you to bless me with a full awakening of my senses, so that I do not miss even one of your heavenly messages. I thank you for conversing with me through your Holy Spirit that dwells inside of me. I love you Father. I love you Jesus. I love you Holy Spirit. I pray all of these things in Jesus Christ's magnificent name. Amen!

# Father, What else do you want me to know, understand, or believe?

# Key #5 RECEIVE DELIVERANCE FOR YOUR SOUL

What I have discovered in my years of being a Christian, and in my years of experience in a Hands-on-Healing prayer ministry, is that there are so many believers who walk around for decades burdened and imprisoned by their past, even if they are diligent in reading their Bible, going to church, and spending quality time with Yahweh praying and listening for his majestic voice.

Therefore, I cannot stress enough how important it is for all believers to receive deliverance and inner healing from a trained Christian deliverance minister, in order to help them cleanse their soul of past traumas, unclean spirits, unforgiveness, bitterness, addictions, generational curses, spiritual wounds, ungodly soul ties, etc.

I look at deliverance as a great way of jumpstarting your sanctification process of cleansing your soul of your worldly ways and worldly baggage!

I also personally know how extremely important deliverance is for believers, because I have experienced first-hand what deliverance accomplishes. A few years ago, I met with a deliverance minister, because Yahweh wanted me to know what it was like. I obeyed Yahweh's request, even though I didn't think I needed deliverance, because my life was already abundant.

All I can say is, "**WOW... I SO NEEDED TO BE DELIVERED!**"

I ended up spending eight hours with a very talented deliverance team who addressed traumas I hadn't thought about for decades. When these traumas were brought to the surface of my mind and heart, and then addressed, I knew without a doubt that Yahweh was thoroughly cleansing me of my past. For I knew that Yahweh desired for me to be delivered of every unclean demonic spirit that was unknowingly influencing me, so I could experience **COMPLETE FREEDOM**, and no longer be held back from my destiny in Yahweh's kingdom.

Yahweh always reminds me, "**MY PEOPLE PERISH FOR A LACK OF KNOWLEDGE**" (Hosea 4:6), and he is so right.

        WWW.JUDYJACOBSONMINISTRIES.com

What I realized from this experience is that you don't know what you don't know. That is why it is so important to see an experienced deliverance minister soon after your salvation, so that your soul can be freed from **ANY and ALL** unclean spirits that have you **KNOWINGLY and UNKNOWINGLY** spiritually bound.

Let Yahweh lead you to who he would want to pray over you for deliverance. For only Yahweh knows who he has **CALLED and GIFTED** for this purpose, to set his children's souls free from demonic influence.

**Luke 4:31-36**
And he (Jesus) came down to Capernaum, a city of Galilee, and he was teaching them on the Sabbath; and they were amazed at his teaching, for his message was with authority. In the synagogue there was a man possessed by the spirit of an unclean demon, and he cried out with a loud voice, "Let us alone! What business do we have with each other, Jesus of Nazareth? Have you come to destroy us? I know who you are, the Holy One of God!" But Jesus rebuked him, saying, "Be quiet and come out of him!" And when the demon had thrown him down in the midst of the people, he came out of him without doing him any harm. And amazement came upon them all, and they began talking with one another saying, **"WHAT IS THIS WORD? FOR WITH AUTHORITY AND POWER HE COMMANDS THE UNCLEAN SPIRITS AND THEY COME OUT."**

**Mark 16:17-18**
"And these signs will accompany those who believe: **IN MY NAME** they will **CAST OUT DEMONS**; they will speak in new tongues; ... they will **LAY THEIR HANDS ON THE SICK**, and they will recover.

# 5 Key Deliverance

**KEY #5 QUESTIONS:**

Satan has convinced a large majority of Christians that if you are a believer in Jesus Christ you cannot be possessed or oppressed by a demon. He wants you to believe that once you received the Holy Spirit, that you are completely sealed from demons. I can tell you, after praying over many Christians, that this belief is absolutely false. Just by using common sense, it becomes obvious that the **SOULS** of Christians are often influenced by spirits of anger, fear, pride, insecurity, abandonment, arrogance, addiction, infirmity, torment, anxiety, depression, suicide, religion, etc. Therefore, not only is it important to understand how demons operate in influencing the souls of believers, but it is also important to receive deliverance from these demons that could possibly have been operating in your life for decades.

Father, what traumas in my life have opened doors to demons?

_____

_____

_____

Father, what demons are currently influencing me?

_____

_____

_____

_____

Father, do I have any ungodly soul ties that need to be severed?

_____

_____

_____

_____

I highly recommend reading the book titled, "**When Pigs Move In: How to sweep clean the demonic influences impacting your life and the lives of others**," by Don Dickerman.

**PRAYER:** Heavenly Father, thank you for desiring to set me completely free from all of the baggage of my past. I thank you Jesus for dying on the cross for my sins, so that I could not only be forgiven of my sins, but also so that I could be set free from all of the demons that are currently trying to kill steal and destroy my life. Father, please give me the knowledge and the wisdom to know how to first close the doors to these demons, and then completely cleanse myself of them. Thank you for gifting your children with the power and authority of Jesus to cast out demons and to heal the sick, so that we too can walk as Jesus walked, setting free all who are oppressed by the devil. I pray all of these things in Jesus's powerful name. Amen!

# Father, What else do you want me to know, understand, or believe?

# Key #6  Know Thy Enemy Satan

Did you know we have the same Holy Spirit within us that Jesus had in him, while he walked on earth in human form? It's true...no more and no less. So why is it most Christians walk around so defeated and oppressed, not looking much different than most non-believers?

**THERE ARE THREE REASONS:**

**1.** You have seriously **UNDERESTIMATED** the power of the Holy Spirit given in Jesus' name living within you.

**2.** You have **OVERESTIMATED** the power of Yahweh's adversary, Satan, and therefore don't use the Holy Spirit's power within you to defeat him.

**3.** You are **UNEDUCATED** to Satan's deceptive ways and are therefore unknowingly handing over your power to him daily.

So who exactly is Satan? Let me give you a quick history lesson.

The Bible calls Satan by many different names. In fact, except for Jesus Christ, there are more names for Satan in the Bible than for anyone else. Satan, Devil, Adversary, Beast, Abaddon, Beelzebub, Apollyon, Antichrist, Deceiver, Dragon, Enemy, Murderer, Tempter, Accuser, Thief, Serpent of Old, Ruler of this world ... the list goes on! Each of Satan's names adds a little more to the description of how evil he actually is. But life for Satan as the king of the bottomless pit was not always like this. Satan, at one point in creation, had a different name and a different position in God's kingdom. The book of Isaiah tells us that Yahweh once described Satan as "**DAY STAR**, **SON OF DAWN!**" And, the book of Ezekiel describes his former beauty...

"**You were the signet of perfection, full of wisdom and perfect in beauty**. You were in Eden, the garden of God; every precious stone was your covering, carnelian, topaz, and jasper, chrysolite, beryl, and onyx, sapphire, carbuncle, and emerald; and wrought in gold were your settings and your engravings. On the day that you were created they were prepared. With an anointed guardian cherub I placed you; you were on the holy mountain of God; in the midst of the stones of fire you walked. **You were blameless in your ways from the day you were created, till iniquity was found in you.**" (Ezekiel 28:12b–15)

At one time, Satan was a beautiful angel. His name was Day Star, which referred to the morning star and literally meant, "bringer of dawn." He ushered in the morning light from the darkness. Yahweh created him as the seal of perfection, a perfect creation, full of beauty and wisdom. He was adorned in precious stones and gold. He walked where Yahweh walked. Day Star's position was one of the highest possible for angels. Scripture tells us he was one of the two guardian cherubs that covered the throne of Yahweh.

Day after day, Day Star overshadowed the throne of Yahweh with his wings, while his face never turned away from God. Life couldn't have been any better for this angel—of course until the day Yahweh removed Day Star's light and he was cast down to the earth.

"**How you are fallen from heaven, O Day Star, son of Dawn!** How you are cut down to the ground, you who laid the nations low! You said in your heart, 'I will ascend to heaven; above the stars of God I will set my throne on high; I will sit on the mount of assembly in the far north; I will ascend above the heights of the clouds, I will make myself like the Most High.'" (Isaiah 14:12–14)

"**Your heart was proud because of your beauty**; you corrupted your wisdom for the sake of your splendor. I cast you to the ground." (Ezekiel 28:17a)

This mighty angel grew proud because of his beauty. Satan became envious of Yahweh's position and his power in the universe and wanted it for himself. Satan's heart had become hard. Even though he already was the most perfect reflection of Yahweh's glory, it wasn't enough. He wanted more. In the beginning, Day Star had an intimate relationship with Yahweh and Jesus, but he was still dissatisfied. He wanted to be God and have all his glory. Day Star wanted his own glory so he could sit on the very throne that he was created to protect. So, Day Star rebelled against his Creator. Therefore, it is not surprising that Jesus tells us he "saw Satan fall like lightning from heaven" (Luke 10:18). Once he was cast to the ground along with all the other rebellious angels, Day Star was given a new name: "They have as king over them the angel of the bottomless pit; his name in Hebrew is Abad'don, and in Greek he is called Apol'lyon" (Revelation 9:11).

From that time forward, Satan, Devil, Abaddon, and Apollyon would forever be his names. The original Hebrew word Satan means "adversary." Devil is translated from the Greek word "diabolos," Diabolos means "an accuser, a slanderer." The words Abaddon and Apollyon mean "ruin and destruction." The angel who used to usher in light from the darkness was now only capable of producing darkness. There was no more God-given light left in Day Star. Because of his own choices, Satan now only had the power of being the destroyer of people's lives. His new names reflected his new position in the universe as being Yahweh's adversary, enemy, and opponent.

# Key 6 🔑 The Disguise

When you think about Satan's former life as Day Star, you know that **HIS FACE** was always turned **TOWARDS** Yahweh. And because of Day Star's close proximity to the throne, every time Yahweh spoke, Satan heard his voice **LOUD AND CLEAR**. What Day Star also witnessed firsthand is the **POWER** of Yahweh's majestic voice. When Yahweh spoke, the angels first listened and then carried out Yahweh's will. In addition, Day Star saw supernatural events take place when Yahweh spoke, like the entire earth being created out of nothing.

Once Satan turned his face away from Yahweh and was kicked out of heaven, his new goal was to become the ruler of this world. He decided he would do whatever it took to get the "humans" Yahweh created to **LISTEN TO HIS VOICE**, instead of Yahweh's, so that he would have his desired power over Yahweh's creation. In order to do this, he would have to keep men's faces turned away from God, and far from him, so they could not hear Yahweh's voice for themselves. If he could keep them from hearing or reading Yahweh's truth, then the only **LOUD VOICE** in their lives would be his, giving him the ultimate power over their lives. Satan knew the only way he would be successful is by being very deceitful and sneaky. He would have to go into the world in a disguise, and he would have to teach his fellow demons how to do this as well.

Satan could think of no better way of disguising himself than as an angel of light. Even he knew no one would be fooled into following an angel of darkness, the one and only angel of death. He had to make the world believe he was someone else. Satan used to be Day Star, son of Dawn. From his previous life he used to usher in the morning light. Even though there was no more God-given light left in him, he would have to fake it.

What an awesome plan! He would become the master of disguises. It was such a great plan, because Satan knew that deceived people do not know they are being deceived. Once people are deceived, they start making really bad decisions on their own. The resulting consequences of their choices bring these individuals even further down into misery. They become so depressed by their circumstances that a relationship with Yahweh is far from their minds.

Deception is like receiving a counterfeit one hundred dollar bill. It is specifically designed to look very much like an authentic bill. The creator of the counterfeit bill knows that **UNTRAINED EYES** will just key in on the many similarities of what they know a one hundred dollar bill looks like and accept it as being real. So unless the receivers have knowledge of the slight differences between the two and are trained to see them, they will miss the clues. They will be deceived and left with the fake.

Satan is a master of this kind of deception! He knows how to fool man with his lies in every area of society, by making them look like truth. He presents sin to us as something attractive, pleasing, desirable, and beautiful. He presents false teachings as new, enlightening, healing, and life-changing. He calls his lies New Age Spirituality. He covers his lies with beautiful wrapping paper and bows and presents them to the world. It is only after someone accepts one of Satan's lies as truth, unwraps Satan's beautiful present and starts living by them, that they find themselves living in the darkness they were trying to avoid.

The experts who recognize a counterfeit bill are individuals who spend an incredible amount of time studying with great detail an actual one hundred dollar bill. They don't study counterfeits; they know that the best way to detect a counterfeit is to study the real thing. They know that **ONLY** by studying the **REAL THING** will they recognize a **FAKE** when they see it. Therefore, the best way for you to detect Satan's lies is to spend a great amount of time studying the truth, Yahweh's truth. The first step in studying the truth is to keep your face always turned upwards toward Yahweh, so you are so close to your Heavenly Father that when he speaks to you, you will hear him clearly.

In a nutshell, because Satan hates Yahweh, Jesus, and Yahweh's children, his scheme is and always will be to do whatever it takes to keep Yahweh's children from **ENGAGING with the HOLY SPIRIT** within them, so that they will not create an intimate relationship with Yahweh or Jesus, know his wisdom and truth, their powerful and rich identity in Jesus Christ, or their inheritance, thereby **HINDERING or DESTROYING** the abundant life that Jesus came to give them.

**John 8:44**
He (Satan) was a murderer from the beginning, and has nothing to do with the truth, because there is no truth in him. When he lies, he speaks according to his own nature, for **HE IS A LIAR and the FATHER OF LIES**.

**2 Corinthians 11:14**
"...for even Satan **DISGUISES** himself as an angel of light."

**1 Peter 5:8**
"Be sober, be watchful. Your adversary the devil **PROWLS AROUND** like a roaring lion, seeking someone to **DEVOUR**."

**John 10:10**
"The thief (Satan) comes only to **STEAL** and **KILL** and **DESTROY**; I (Jesus) came that they may have **LIFE**, and have it **ABUNDANTLY**."

**KEY #6 QUESTIONS:**

Father, what am I currently believing about **MYSELF** that is a **LIE** from Satan?

_____
_____
_____
_____
_____
_____

Father, what **TRUTH** about **MYSELF** do you want me to believe?

_____
_____
_____
_____
_____
_____

Father, what am I currently believing about **YOU** that is a **LIE** from Satan?

_____
_____
_____
_____
_____
_____
_____

Father, what **TRUTH** about **YOU** do you want me to believe?

_____
_____
_____
_____
_____
_____
_____

Father, what am I currently believing about (**A PERSON OR SITUATION**) that is a **LIE** from Satan? Father, what is your **TRUTH**?

_____
_____
_____
_____
_____
_____
_____
_____
_____
_____
_____

Father, who do you say that I am?

_____
_____
_____
_____
_____
_____
_____
_____

**PRAYER:** Heavenly Father, thank you for **TRUTH**, as I know only your truth with set me free from all the schemes of the enemy Satan. Please forgive me for all of the times I have turned my face away from you and walked away from your truth. Father, when I give you my time, by entering into your Presence daily, I ask that you give me your heavenly wisdom in all areas of my life. As I turn my face towards you, I give you permission to make aware of my blind spots that only you can see. I ask for you to show me all the ways I am being deceived by the enemy. Show me how to fully walk in your bright light, instead of Satan's darkness. Thank you Jesus for being the **WAY**, the **TRUTH**, and the **LIFE**. I desire to walk your narrow path from this day forward! I pray all of these things in Jesus Christ's exalted name. Amen!

# Father, What else do you want me to know, understand, or believe?

# Key #7 Stop Aiding and Abetting the Enemy

One morning I woke up to Yahweh saying in my Spirit, "**AIDING AND ABETTING**." I wasn't sure if these words were for me, or the woman our ministry team was soon going to pray for. It wasn't long before it became apparent who Yahweh's words were for.

Within minutes of meeting the woman we were praying for that morning, it became painfully obvious she was not in a good place physically, emotionally, or spiritually. Unfortunately, Satan had been robbing this woman of **ALL** peace, love, joy, and abundant living. It was evident she had been imprisoned by the enemy for a very long time. She had asked us to pray for her because she was desperate to escape her "**JAIL CELL**."

So, our ministry team did what Yahweh always led us to do during our prayer sessions. We started teaching this lady about communication with God through the Holy Spirit. We discussed how to listen to, and how to hear, Yahweh's majestic voice through the Bible, dreams, visions, words of knowledge, creation, prophecy, etc. We discussed how important it is to receive the Baptism of the Holy Spirit, and how and why praying in tongues regularly will empower you. We stressed that by daily entering into Yahweh's presence you will gain wisdom, knowledge, understanding, revelation, insight, and counsel from your heavenly Counselor. It is during your time with Yahweh that he can deposit into you everything you need, in order to prepare you for what the world will throw at you on any given day.

Our conversation with this woman was one we frequently have with the people we pray for. But what was different about this conversation is this woman informed us that she had already received the Baptism of the Holy Spirit, and her gift of tongues a long time ago. She also had frequent dreams and visions that she knew were messages from Yahweh, and she knew how to clearly hear his precious voice. She told us about all of her old journals that documented her previous conversations with her Creator. So...why did she need us to pray for her? Why was her life in such shambles?

That's when Yahweh reminded me of the words I woke up to: "**AIDING AND ABETTING**." What I quickly realized is that she was aiding and abetting the enemy in her life by not using what she had been given by her Lord and Savior to utilize.

"Aiding and abetting" are terms used in criminal law, which mean that another person helped the primary person do whatever criminal act for which they are charged. Aiding or abetting can vary from driving a car, to being present at a fight and rendering assistance, or being a lookout for a burglary or robbery or any other crime. If a person is convicted of aiding or abetting, they are convicted for the same level of crime, in which they assisted, as the person who actually pulled the trigger or did the burglary.

      www.JUDYJACOBSONMINISTRIES.com

Unfortunately, Yahweh wanted me to know that this woman was just as responsible as Satan for her state of being. The circumstantial evidence was strong. Even though she had learned a long time ago how to hear Yahweh's precious voice, she admitted that she was spending **ZERO TIME IN HIS PRESENCE**, in order to hear what he had to say. Even though she knew how to analyze and journal her dreams, visions, and conversations with Yahweh for their messages, she was not taking the time to do so. Even though she had her gift of speaking in tongues, which scripture tells us is for the purpose of edifying yourself, she wasn't using this God given gift to recharge her batteries. To add to it, she wasn't reading her Bible, or devotionals, wasn't praising or worshiping Yahweh, or going to church. She was not receiving what God had to offer her, because she rarely went into his presence to collect all the blessings and counsel he desired to give her.

Talk about aiding and abetting the enemy! This precious woman was living like she was an unbeliever! With absolutely zero communication with Yahweh, she was living through her flesh. As a result, her life reflected all that comes with living in the world, because she wasn't inviting Yahweh into it. Because of her choosing to live in the flesh, instead of her Spirit, the enemy easily came and set up residence in her **THOUGHTS AND MIND**. Her circumstances, her actions, and the words that came out of her mouth, were proof Satan had a stronghold, a death grip, upon her. By not spending time with Yahweh listening to his voice, journalling and analyzing her dreams and visions, spending quiet time in praise and worship, and praying in tongues, she was helping the enemy **STEAL HER LIFE** out from under her.

What was interesting is that nothing we told her about spending time with the Lord in order to receive her daily manna was news to her. She understood the importance about everything we discussed. She just wasn't putting in the effort. She readily admitted she wasn't sacrificing her time to enter into Yahweh's Presence, so he could renew her mind, her thoughts, her actions, her desires, her will. Unfortunately, this woman had given into the **SPIRIT OF LAZINESS**. She had become part of what God calls the **SLACKER GENERATION**. How unfortunate her situation was, when she had all she needed within her to turn her circumstances around.

This woman's situation was a direct result of **ENGAGING WITH THE SPIRITS OF SATAN'S WORLD**, instead of engaging with the Holy Spirit. Because of her choices, she was severely grieving and quenching the Holy Spirit within her, and therefore not benefitting from the Holy Spirit's living waters flowing through her.

A few days after this prayer session, Yahweh woke me up to the following words in order to confirm his message...

**"YOU ARE AIDING AND ABETTING THE ENEMY WHEN...YOU DON'T TAKE YOUR SHOES OFF!"**

# 7 Key

## Take your shoes off

I just love the way Yahweh speaks. It took me a moment before I understood what he was saying. Do you remember when Yahweh spoke to Moses out of a burning bush? The first thing he told Moses to do was to remove his shoes, because the place Moses was standing was on holy ground. The ground was holy, because Yahweh's Holy Presence was before Moses. I believe God asked Moses to take his shoes off as a symbolic gesture of removing the dirt of the world from his feet. Yahweh would only talk to Moses if Moses agreed to leave the physical worldly realm and enter into Yahweh's spiritual realm, if only for a moment.

Therefore, when you **DON'T** take your shoes off, it means you are not entering into God's Presence. Yahweh's words to me were a very creative way of saying, **"YOU ARE AIDING AND ABETTING THE ENEMY WHEN...YOU DON'T SPEND TIME WITH ME."** By not taking time out of your day to spend with Yahweh you are choosing not to be encouraged, renewed, empowered, restored, inspired, rejuvenated. By doing this, in essence you are instead choosing to let the enemy have his way with you.

So, my question to you is this, **"ARE YOU AIDING AND ABETTING THE ENEMY**?" As harsh as it may sound, you may be just as liable as Satan for your circumstances, by not giving your Lord and Savior your time.

Your circumstances will let you know if you are aiding and abetting the enemy. It's easy to detect. Are you consumed by what Satan and his demons are doing in your life? Do you have daily battles taking place in your mind and thoughts? Do you have trouble determining the truth from a lie? Have your demons become so familiar that they hang out with you regularly, speaking into your ear? Are you spiritually consuming what they have to offer? Do they captivate your attention? Do you suffer from anxiety, depression, sadness, turmoil? Are you a mess? Do you lack peace, love and joy?

Well, it's time to stop helping the enemy in his quest to steal, kill and destroy your life. It's time to boot Satan out of your presence and invite Yahweh into it! It's time to use your power and authority, as a precious child of God, to command Satan to leave your home, thoughts, and heart immediately. Speak to him out loud! Tell him he is no longer welcome. Inform him you are no longer going to render assistance in his schemes against you and your life, and you are going to take back your dominion.

Then curse the spirit of laziness. In Jesus' name, command it to the pit, never to return. Make a commitment to sacrifice your time to your Lord and Savior. Meet with him daily! Receive you daily bread: revelations from heaven, strategies to defeat your personal demons, Yahweh's will for your life, daily instructions of how to handle tough situations, wisdom, knowledge, understanding...

If you meet with Yahweh regularly, it is guaranteed you will be victorious and will be released from the personal prison that currently has you bound, because Jesus came to set the captives free! Your soul will be so filled to overflowing with the Holy Spirit's **LIVING WATERS** of peace, love and joy, there won't be room for Satan or his demons. They will be forced to flee! Hallelujah!!!

**James 4:7**
"**SUBMIT** yourselves therefore to God. **RESIST** the devil and he will flee from you."

**Matthew 4:4**
"Man shall not **LIVE** by bread alone, **BUT BY EVERY WORD** that proceeds from the mouth of the Lord."

**Revelation 3:15-22**
"I know your works: you are neither cold nor hot. Would that you were cold or hot! So, because you are **LUKEWARM**, and neither cold nor hot, **I WILL SPEW YOU OUT OF MY MOUTH**. For you say, I am rich, I have prospered, and I need nothing; not knowing that you are wretched, pitiable, poor, blind, and naked. Therefore I counsel you to buy from me gold refined by fire, that you may be rich, and white garments to clothe you and to keep the shame of your nakedness from being seen, and salve to anoint your eyes, that you may see. Those whom I love, I reprove and chasten; so be zealous and **REPENT**. Behold, **I STAND AT THE DOOR AND KNOCK**; if any one hears my voice and opens the door, I will come in to him and eat with him, and he with me. He who conquers, I will grant him to sit with me on my throne, as I myself conquered and sat down with my Father on his throne. He who has an ear, let him hear what the Spirit says to the churches."

**Galatians 5:1**
For freedom Christ has **SET US FREE**; stand fast therefore, and do not submit again to a **YOKE OF SLAVERY**.

**Galatians 5:16**
But I say, **WALK BY THE SPIRIT**, and do not gratify the desires of the flesh.

**KEY #7 QUESTIONS:**
Father, how am I currently being deceived by Satan?

_____
_____
_____
_____

Father, how have I specifically aided and abetted the enemy in my past?

_____
_____
_____
_____

Father, how am I currently aiding and abetting the enemy in my life?

_____
_____
_____
_____
_____

Father, in what areas of my life am I lukewarm?

_____
_____
_____
_____
_____

**PRAYER:** Heavenly Father, please forgive me for all the times that I have aided and abetted the enemy in my life. I repent for all the times I blamed you for my circumstances, as I did not see how I was playing a part in my imprisonment and bondage. Please forgive me for my laziness of not spending time with you, studying your Word, listening for and obeying your voice, or journaling the dreams, visions or words that you gave me. Thank you for knocking with persistence at the door of my heart Jesus. I open that door to you today, and give you my time. I also give your Holy Spirit within me full access to my soul from this day forward. Father, I want to live the rest of my life with an all-consuming passion for you and your son Jesus. Thank you for always pursuing me. I pray all of this in Jesus's loving name. Amen!

# Father, What else do you want me to know, understand, or believe?

# Key #8 Pick up your Sword of the Spirit

SPIRIT

"In the beginning was the Word, and the Word was with God, and the Word was God... **AND THE WORD (JESUS) BECAME FLESH AND DWELT AMONG US**, full of grace and truth; we have beheld his glory, glory as of the only Son from the Father." (John 1:1,14)

"Do not think that I have come to bring peace on earth; I (Jesus) have not come to bring peace, **BUT A SWORD**." (Matthew 10:34)

"And **TAKE** the helmet of salvation, and the **SWORD OF THE SPIRIT** which is the **WORD OF GOD**." (Ephesians 6:17)

While Jesus walked on earth, he walked fully human, with Yahweh's Holy Spirit dwelling inside of him. 2 Peter 5-8 says, "Have this in mind among yourselves...though he was in the form of God, did not count equality with God a thing to be grasped, but emptied himself, taking the form of a servant, being born in the **LIKENESS OF MEN**."

We know that Jesus, being born to a human mother (Matthew 1:25), experienced hunger (Matthew 21:18) and thirst (John 19:28). He bled (John 19:34), he cried (John 11:35), and he died (John 19:30). He experienced temptation (Matthew 4:1), and yet he did not sin (Hebrews 4:15). No deceit was found on his lips (1 Peter 2:22).

So how did Jesus do it? How did he live a human life for 33 years without once sinning, through his thoughts, actions or words? In short, Jesus engaged with Yahweh's Holy Spirit inside of him on a daily basis. That is the only way Jesus could have remained sinless, while living on planet earth. Jesus gives us a clue of how he accomplished this amazing feat on two occasions by the words he spoke.

The first occasion occurred when Mary and Joseph lost Jesus when he was 12 years old (Luke 2:41-52). Mary and Joseph had just left Jerusalem after celebrating the feast of Passover. One day into their journey home, they realized they hadn't seen Jesus for a while. They asked around, but no one knew where he was. When they did not find him, they returned to Jerusalem **SEEKING HIM**! When they finally found Jesus in the Temple they said to him, "Son, why have you treated us so? Behold your father and I have been looking for you anxiously." Jesus replied,
**"DID YOU NOT KNOW THAT I MUST BE IN MY FATHER'S HOUSE?"**

So much significance can be found in Jesus's first words written in the Bible. Obviously, Jesus wasn't talking about the physical temple where his parents found him. Instead, he was expressing that his favorite place in the whole world was in his Heavenly Father's Presence. You see Jesus entered into his Father's House through the Holy Spirit within him daily. Jesus knew it is in his Father's Presence where he **BELONGED**, and where he could receive his daily bread: truth, wisdom, understanding, knowledge, revelation, insight, strategy, encouragement, instructions, purpose, provision, strength, peace, love, and joy. It was in his Father's House where he could find the answer to every one of his questions. It was in his Father's Presence where he learned the secrets of Yahweh's Kingdom, of which he was an heir, as Yahweh's beloved Son.

I can imagine Jesus saying to Mary and Joseph, "Haven't you noticed how much time I spend reading Scripture, praying, and listening for our Heavenly Father's voice? Haven't you ever wondered why I don't have the same sin issues as my brothers and sisters do? It's because I am always in constant communication with my Father, receiving answers to my questions, and finding out what my Father would do or say in every one of my situations, before I act or speak. For my Heavenly Father leads and guides me daily."

Scripture says that Mary and Joseph didn't understand what Jesus was saying, because they didn't have the Holy Spirit within them, and therefore did not comprehend that Jesus had been **WALKING SPIRIT-LED** his entire life.

Jesus confirms what he said to his parents as a teenager, during his ministry, when he says to the people, "Truly, truly, I say to you, the Son can do nothing of his own accord, but **ONLY WHAT HE SEES THE FATHER DOING**; for whatever he does, that the Son does likewise" (John 5:19-20). "For I have not spoken on my own authority, the Father who sent me has himself given me commandment **WHAT TO SAY AND WHAT TO SPEAK**. And I know that his commandment is eternal life. What I say, therefore, **I SAY AS THE FATHER HAS BIDDEN ME**." (John 12:49-50).

What Jesus was confirming is that he was successful in remaining sinless his entire life, with no deceit on his lips, by **ONLY DOING** what he saw his Father doing, and **ONLY SAYING** what he heard his Father saying. Nothing more and nothing less.

Jesus shows us exactly how he came against the enemy's temptations day after day after day, when he was led into the wilderness by the Holy Spirit after his baptism. For it was in the wilderness that Jesus showed us **HOW** to pick up the Word of God and **USE IT**. Three times Satan came at Jesus tempting him to sin. Three times Jesus responded to Satan's temptations by speaking out loud Yahweh's truth. Three times Jesus shut Satan down with the Sword of the Spirit, which sent Satan fleeing from his presence.

Not only did Jesus **KNOW** Yahweh's Word inside and out, from all of his time spent in his Father's House and Presence, but he also knew the **POWER** of Yahweh's Word, and how to use his Father's powerful truth against the lies and deceptions of the enemy.

# Key 8

## Two-Edged

For Jesus knew, "The truth will set you free, only if you **APPLY** Yahweh's Truth to every single situation you find yourself in." It is when we apply Yahweh's Word, by speaking it out loud, that his word becomes a sword against our enemy.

Hebrews 4:12 says, **"For the WORD OF GOD** is living and active, **SHARPER than any (physical) TWO-EDGED SWORD,** piercing to the division of soul and spirit, of joints and marrow, and discerning the thoughts and intentions of the heart. Revelations 1:16 says, "in his right hand he (Jesus) held seven stars, **FROM HIS MOUTH** issued a sharp **TWO-EDGED SWORD,** and his face was like the sun shining in full strength."

The phrase "two-edged" is taken from the Greek word "distomos" and is unquestionably one of the oddest words in the entire New Testament. Why is it so odd? Because it is a compound of the word "di", meaning "two," and the word "stomos," which is the Greek word for one's mouth. Thus, when these two words are compounded into one "distomos," they describe something that is **TWO-MOUTHED!** That seems strange. Why would the Bible refer to the Word of God repeatedly as a "two-edged sword" or, literally, a "two-mouthed sword"?

Ephesians 6:17 advises us to **TAKE UP** the Sword of the Spirit, which is the Word of God. But what does that look like?

Here's how you do it. Let's say you are praying about a situation, and suddenly a Bible verse rises up from inside your heart. At that moment, you are consciously aware that Yahweh has given you a verse to stand on and to claim for your situation. You've received a word that came right out of the mouth of Yahweh and dropped into your spirit! His word is so sharp that it cuts right through your questions, intellect, and natural logic and lodges deep within your heart as truth.

After you meditate on that quickened word from Yahweh, it suddenly begins to release its power inside you. Soon you can't contain it any longer! Everything within you wants to **DECLARE** what God has said to you. You want to **RELEASE IT** out of your mouth. And when you do, those powerful words are sent forth like a mighty blade to drive back the forces of hell that had been marshaled against you, your family, your business, your ministry, your finances, your relationship, or your body.

# Sword of the Spirit

The Word of God remains a one-bladed sword when it comes out of Yahweh's mouth and drops into your heart, but is never released from your own mouth by faith. That supernatural word simply lies dormant in your heart, never becoming the two-edged sword Yahweh designed it to be. But something happens in the realm of the Spirit when you finally rise up and begin to speak forth that word. The moment it comes out of your mouth, a second edge is added to the blade!

Nothing is more powerful than a word that comes first from Yahweh's mouth and then from your mouth. It means you and Yahweh have come into agreement with his truth, and that agreement releases his mighty power into the situation at hand! It became a sharp, "two-edged," or literally, a "two-mouthed" sword that can be used against the enemy.

That is why it is so important to read Yahweh's Word on a daily basis. Yahweh's Word can only be used against the enemy, if you have first placed Yahweh's Word in your heart for later use. The first edge is placed on the sword by first reading and then believing Yahweh's Word is the absolute truth. Then when you are confronted by a challenge from the demonic realm, the Holy Spirit will be able to reach down into the reservoir of God's Word you have stored up in your heart and pull up the exact scripture you need for that moment. That is when Yahweh's Word becomes a two-edged sword and is when the demons start to tremble in terror and flee from your presence.

Remember Jesus said, "Do not think that I have come to bring peace on earth; I have not come to bring peace, **BUT A SWORD**." What this means is that Jesus came first to bring us the **WORD OF GOD** and then to teach us how to use the Word of God as a sword against our enemy. By wielding the sword Jesus has given us against our enemy, peace is brought into our mind, our emotions, our soul, our family, our home.

This kingdom principle, or what Jesus calls a **KEY TO THE KINGDOM**, is portrayed in God's Word. Matthew 16:19 says, "I (Jesus) will give you the keys of the kingdom of heaven, and whatever you **BIND** on earth shall be **BOUND** in heaven, and whatever you **LOOSE** on earth shall be **LOOSED** in heaven."

# What Jesus gives believers

Jesus gives believers the power to **BIND** all of the schemes of the enemy, and all of his demons in their lives, when Yahweh's powerful Word is spoken out of our mouths.

He also gives us the power to **LOOSE** all of the blessings of heaven by declaring Yahweh's powerful Word over our lives. When we wield the Sword of the Spirit, in Jesus's mighty name, against Satan's demons and their lies, I envision Yahweh's angels escorting them to the pit of hell and binding them in chains forever. In addition, when we loosen God's goodness from heaven, in Jesus's mighty name, I envision heaven's mighty angels carrying Yahweh's blessings, grace, mercy, restoration, provision, and all of the fruits and gifts of the Holy Spirit, from heaven to his children on earth.

> "
>
> ### Satan knows that believers have the **POWER**

Satan knows that believers have the power to bind and loose with Yahweh's Word. Therefore, in order to prevent Yahweh's powerful kingdom principle from being utilized, Satan will try to keep you from seeing his deceptive work in your life. Remember Satan is a master of lies and deception and disguises himself as an angel of light. That is why it becomes critical to go to Yahweh frequently in order to ask him questions such as, "How am I currently being deceived?", "What lies or false beliefs am I believing?", "Show me the traumas or offenses that have me bound.", "Why am I giving into temptation?", "What would you do in my situation?", "Show me what is truly going on in the spiritual realm.", "How would you respond to what was said?", "Show me my sins.", "Show me strategy on how to defeat the enemy **WITH YOUR WORD**."

Trust me when I say, when you ask Yahweh these questions, he is sure to answer because he knows **ONLY HIS TRUTH** has the **POWER** to set the captives **FREE**!

Therefore, take every thought captive and present it to Yahweh in order to discover his truth in every matter, like Jesus did, before you act or speak. For we pull down and destroy all strongholds in our life, our families, our homes, our workplaces, neighborhoods and nations, when we destroy Satan's lies and deception with the Word of God.

Proverbs 20:12 says, "The hearing ear, and the seeing eye, Yahweh has made them both." Because the Holy Spirit dwells within Yahweh's children, all believers in Jesus Christ have a spiritual hearing ear and a seeing eye. What that means is we all have the potential to live our lives like Jesus did, by only doing what we see our Father doing and only saying what we hear our Father saying.

So enter into your Father's Presence, into your Father's House, often, and you are guaranteed to live the abundant life!

Like a lion, Satan is only successful in devouring the weak. Therefore, as Yahweh's people we need to recognize the power within us, rise up, stand our ground, and tell Satan with our God given authority, **"NO MORE!"**

*It's time to take back what Satan has Stolen*

**Matthew 10:1**

And he called to him his twelve disciples and **GAVE THEM AUTHORITY** over unclean spirits, to cast them out, and to heal every disease and every infirmity.

**Luke 10:19**

"Behold, I have **GIVEN YOU AUTHORITY** to tread upon serpents and scorpions, and **OVER ALL THE POWER OF THE ENEMY**; and nothing shall hurt you."

**Isaiah 54:17**

"**NO WEAPON** that is fashioned against you **SHALL PROSPER**, and you shall confute every tongue that rises against you in judgment. This is the heritage of the servants of Yahweh and their vindication from me, says Yahweh."

**2 Corinthians 10:4-5**

For the weapons of our warfare are not of the flesh but have **DIVINE POWER** to destroy strongholds. We destroy arguments and every lofty opinion raised against the knowledge of God, and **TAKE EVERY THOUGHT CAPTIVE** to obey Christ,

**1 John 4:4**

**"For HE WHO IS IN YOU is GREATER than he who is in the world."**

**Ephesians 6:10-18**

"Finally, be strong in the Lord and in the strength of his might. **PUT ON THE WHOLE ARMOR OF GOD**, that you may be able to stand against the wiles of the devil. For we are not contending against flesh and blood, but against the principalities, against the powers, against the world rulers of this present darkness, against the spiritual hosts of wickedness in the heavenly places. Therefore take the whole armor of God, that you may be able to withstand in the evil day, and having done all, to stand. Stand therefore, having **GIRDED** your loins with **TRUTH**, and having **PUT ON** the breastplate of **RIGHTEOUSNESS**, and having **SHOD** your feet with the **EQUIPMENT** of the gospel of peace; besides all these, **TAKING** the shield of **FAITH**, with which you can quench all the flaming darts of the evil one. And **TAKE** the **HELMET OF SALVATION**, and the **SWORD OF THE SPIRIT** which is the word of God. **PRAY** at all times **IN THE SPIRIT**, with all prayer and supplication."

**KEY #8 QUESTIONS:**
Father, what has Satan stolen from me and my family?

_____

_____

_____

_____

_____

Father, am I wielding the **SWORD OF THE SPIRIT** effectively against the enemy?

_____

_____

_____

_____

_____

_____

Father, bring a situation to my mind where I need to use the Sword of the Spirit. What **WORD** do I need to declare out loud over this situation?

_____

_____

_____

_____

_____

_____

To learn more about your power and authority in Jesus Christ, I highly recommend reading, "**The Believer's Authority: What you didn't learn in Church,**" by Andrew Wommack.

**PRAYER:** Yahweh, I know that your **WORD** has the power to defeat every adversary in my life. As I take it into my heart and get it deep into my soul, I know it will empower me with Jesus's mighty power and authority. Forgive me for the times I have just skimmed over your Word rather than planting it deep into my heart. I realize that the answers I seek are in your Word and that your Word, when spoken from my mouth, releases power against the devices of Satan. So today, Yahweh, I choose to no longer aid and abet the enemy. Instead, I am making the decision right now to start releasing the power of your **TRUTH** against him. Teach me all that I need to know on how to utilize the **SWORD OF THE SPIRIT**, and how to use **YOUR KEY** of binding and loosing, so I can live in freedom and abundance. I pray this all in Jesus's all-powerful name. Amen!

# Father, What else do you want me to know, understand, or believe?

_____
_____
_____
_____
_____
_____
_____
_____
_____
_____
_____
_____
_____
_____
_____
_____
_____
_____
_____
_____
_____
_____
_____
_____
_____
_____
_____

# Key #9 Receive the Baptism of the Holy Spirit

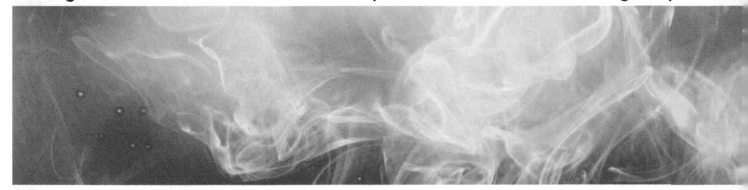

For years now, Yahweh has been speaking to me about the importance of his children coming into complete **UNION** with his Son, Jesus Christ. Yahweh has actually allowed me to feel his heart on the important issue of Christians coming into complete alignment with Jesus's desires for them. For Yahweh knows that unless all of his children come into union with Jesus **FIRST**, unity within the church as a whole, across denominational lines, will never happen.

One Sunday morning, God literally had me cry **HIS TEARS** for 4 hours straight, because a large majority of his children are **NOT** in union with Jesus. In fact, I could not stop Yahweh's tears from flowing through my eyes, until he was done using me. It was something that had never happened to me before, but is an experience I will never forget.

The day I grieved for Yahweh was day 22, following a 21-day fast. During my fast, I had asked God to give me a greater discernment of spirits. I now know my request was granted, because the first thing I felt, on the day I broke my fast, was my Lord and Savior's heart: **HIS SPIRIT**.

On that day, God specifically wanted me to feel the pain he has for his children who are not in union with Jesus, when it comes to Jesus's **DESIRE TO BAPTIZE** them with Yahweh's Holy Spirit and with Fire (Acts 1:5, Matthew 3:11, Mark 1:8, Luke 3:16, John 1:33). God wanted me to feel his pain so that, when I talked about this issue, his urgency and passion would be sensed in my voice.

Yahweh wanted me to feel the pain he feels for his children who are not being fully equipped with **EVERYTHING the HOLY SPIRIT** has to offer them.

Yahweh is grieved that his children are living their lives without **HIS POWER and BOLDNESS** to be Jesus's witnesses to the ends of the earth. And because **ALL FACETS of HIS WORD** are not being fulfilled, all areas of his children's lives are being negatively affected, and his kingdom's effectiveness is suffering as a result.

Something has got to change ... We have got to come into **UNION with Jesus** ...

Before I go any further, I want to stress to you that it doesn't matter what denomination you are, or what your denomination currently believes about the baptism of the Holy Spirit. It doesn't matter what your knowledge or understanding of the baptism of the Holy Spirit is. It doesn't matter if you are a new Christian, or have never even heard of the baptism of the Holy Spirit. What matters is your love for Jesus, and what he wants to **BLESS** you with!

WWW.JUDYJACOBSONMINISTRIES.com

If you love Jesus, and desire a more intimate relationship with him, this message is for you! If you want to fulfill the extravagant dreams Jesus has for you, while on planet earth, this message is for you! If you want to experience an exciting, adventurous, and purpose filled life, this message is for you! If you want to walk on this earth with power, authority, boldness, and courage to be a compelling witness for Jesus, this message is for you! If you have already come into union with Jesus with regards to the baptism of the Holy Spirit, but would like an easy way of describing the importance of it to fellow Christians, this message is for you also! And finally, if you have already decided that the baptism of the Holy Spirit is **NOT** for today's believers, please read this until the end, as God has given me a different way of explaining this extravagant **GIFT** from heaven, and why it is critical for **EVERY** believer in Jesus Christ to receive.

So let's begin...

Before I take you to the day of Pentecost, the day the disciples were **BAPTIZED with the HOLY SPIRIT and with FIRE**, as described in Acts 1 & 2 of the Bible, I want to take you to the day of Jesus's resurrection.

What many Christians don't know is what transpired when Jesus met with his disciples on the evening of his resurrection. It was on this evening that Jesus appeared to his disciples, in order to prove to them he had indeed been raised from the dead. It was on this night that the disciples finally believed everything Jesus had said to them during the previous 3 years of walking in his footsteps. Finally, everything made sense. Jesus, who was crucified and buried just 3 days prior, was **NOW ALIVE** and standing before them.

On this night, the disciples finally believed Jesus was indeed **WHO** he declared he was ... **THE SON OF GOD!**

On the night of Jesus's resurrection, the disciples **BELIEVED**! And because they believed, Jesus gave them what he promised they would receive: the Holy Spirit. Jesus had told his disciples, during the Last Supper, the Holy Spirit would come to them, and dwell **WITHIN** them (John 14:15-17, John 14:26-27, John 16:7-11, John 16:13-15).

Scripture says, "On the evening of that (resurrection) day, the first day of the week... Jesus came and stood among them and said to them, '**PEACE BE WITH YOU**.' When he had said this, he showed them his hands and his side. Then the disciples were glad when they saw the Lord. Jesus said to them again, '**PEACE BE WITH YOU**. As the Father has sent me, even so I send you.' And when he had said this, he breathed on them, and said to them, '**RECEIVE THE HOLY SPIRIT**'" (John 20:19-22).

The night of Jesus's resurrection was the disciple's salvation day. On this night, they received the indwelling of the Holy Spirit within them. They received what Jesus described as **PEACE**. In fact, twice Jesus said, "Peace be with you."

Jesus describes the Holy Spirit as "Peace," (John 14:27, John 20:19-22), the "Spirit of Truth" and the "Counselor," (John 14:15-18, John 14:26, John 16:7-11), a "Teacher," (John 14:26), and as the "Communication Link" between Yahweh and his children (John 16:13-15).

Therefore, on the evening of Jesus's resurrection, because the disciples believed Jesus was the Son of God, who died and rose for their sins, they received the Holy Spirit within them, just like believers do today!!!

The day someone accepts Jesus Christ, as their Lord and Savior, is the day they receive **SALVATION** and the **GIFT of THE HOLY SPIRIT** to reside within them. A person's salvation day is the day they receive Yahweh's gift of peace.

So, if the disciples had already received the Holy Spirit, on the evening of Jesus's resurrection, what were the events that occurred 50 days later on Pentecost all about? Why did Jesus desire to baptize his disciples **WITH** the Holy Spirit (Acts 1:5), and why did John the Baptist prophesy that Jesus would do just that (Matthew 3:11, Mark 1:8, Luke 3:16, John 1:33)?

Didn't the disciples already receive everything they needed on their salvation day?

## APPARENTLY NOT...

From Scripture, we know Jesus walked with his disciples for 40 days after his resurrection, before he ascended into heaven to sit at the right hand of his Father Yahweh. Right before Jesus left this earth, he gave his disciples the following instructions, first spoken in the gospel of Luke and then repeated in Acts.

"Behold, I send the **PROMISE OF MY FATHER** upon you; but **STAY** in the city, **UNTIL** you are **CLOTHED WITH POWER** from on high" (Luke 24:49).

"And while staying with them he charged them not to depart from Jerusalem, but to **WAIT** for the **PROMISE OF THE FATHER**, which he said, 'you heard from me, for John baptized with water, but before many days you shall be baptized **WITH** the Holy Spirit... you shall receive **POWER** when the Holy Spirit has come **UPON** you; and you shall be my witnesses...to the end of the earth'" (Acts 1:3-5, 8).

Interesting...on the day of the disciple's salvation, they received **PEACE**, when Jesus breathed on them and said, "Receive the Holy Spirit." And now, Jesus was promising the disciples **POWER**, through the Baptism of the Holy Spirit and Fire.

## PEACE and POWER!

Sounds like two completely different things to me.

I know without doubt that the Holy Spirit within us brings us personal peace, because the Holy Spirit within us becomes our Counselor, our Teacher, and our Communicator with Yahweh and Jesus. The Holy Spirit within us is the avenue by which we receive our daily bread from heaven, which includes personal insight, promptings, instructions, revelation, direction, and dreams and visions from our Heavenly Father through the myriad of ways in which he speaks.

So, what then is the **POWER** that Jesus desires his disciples to receive, through the baptism of the Holy Spirit and Fire? Well, according to Jesus's own words, we need to receive power for the purpose of being **HIS WITNESSES** to the ends of the earth!

It sounds to me like Jesus was telling his disciples, "You are only going to be compelling and effective witnesses for me if you have **MY POWER**, just like I was a compelling and effective witness for Yahweh, because of **YAHWEH's POWER** that came upon me during my baptism, when the dove from heaven descended upon me and remained." (Luke 3:21-22, John 1:32-33, Acts 10:38)

When the disciples heard Jesus's command to **WAIT** for the Promise of the Father, they had two choices. They could obey Jesus's commands to wait for the more, which Jesus describes as **POWER**. Or ... they could choose to disobey Jesus's command, by immediately going back to their lives, being satisfied with the **PEACE of the HOLY SPIRIT** within them that they had already received on the day of their salvation.

Thankfully, the disciples obeyed Jesus's command and waited for the Promise of the Father, or the **GOOD NEWS** of Jesus Christ would likely have never made it to the ends of the earth. And, the disciples would have had to witness through their own human strength.

Scripture says that after Jesus charged the disciples to wait (which ended up being a total of 10 days), the disciples returned to Jerusalem, went to the upper room where they were staying, and **PRAYED in ONE ACCORD** (Acts 1:12-14).

What that means is the disciples all prayed **IN UNION!!!** What that means is all of the disciples prayed for Jesus's will and desire to be done in their lives. Because they believed wholeheartedly what Jesus said would come true, they all came into agreement with Jesus that they would wait to be baptized with the Holy Spirit and Fire, and as a result would have heavenly power come upon them to be his witnesses.

What I find fascinating is the disciples had no idea what they were waiting for. They didn't have Scripture to read in order to figure out what Jesus meant by his promise of being baptized with the Holy Spirit and Fire, because they were the first to receive this gift. They didn't have a preacher to explain **WHAT** it meant, and **HOW** it would all take place. In fact the term, "baptized with the Holy Spirit and fire," might have been something they only heard once through John the Baptist over 3 years prior.

What I think was very strategic, on God's part, is that he made sure Jesus's mother Mary was amongst the disciples, during their 10 days of waiting. I would imagine that Mary shared with the disciples her powerful testimony, of when the angel Gabriel came to her and told her she would conceive in her womb and bear a son named Jesus (Luke 1:26-38). I would imagine she shared that Gabriel told her the **IMPOSSIBLE** would become **POSSIBLE** when the Holy Spirit came upon her and the power of the Most High overshadowed her.

As we know from Scripture, Mary didn't reply to Gabriel's declaration that she would birth the Son of God by saying, "Gabriel, I think I am going to need more explanation, before I agree to this thing you are telling me that I don't completely understand. What do you mean, the power of the Most High will overshadow me? What are the ramifications of this on my personal life? If I agree to birthing Jesus, the Son of God, how exactly is this going to affect my own dreams and desires?"

No...instead Mary said, "**I AM YOUR HANDMAIDEN. LET IT BE TO ME ACCORDING TO YOUR WORD**."

You see, Mary came into complete union with Yahweh's desire for her, without knowing or understanding all that Yahweh was asking of her. All she knew was she loved the Lord with all of her heart. And she believed Yahweh had her best interests at heart. She therefore **SACRIFICED HER BODY** for his purposes!

No if, and, or but ...**NO LIMITATIONS!**

Because of Mary's testimony, and the fact that Jesus who was dead, was now alive, I can see the disciples coming to the same conclusion as Mary did. I can imagine all the disciples praying in union...

"Jesus, even though we don't know how you are going to accomplish what you are saying, we are your disciples, and we believe what you have told us is true. Therefore, **LET IT BE TO US ACCORDING TO YOUR WORD!** We believe you and want to receive **EVERYTHING** you have for us, through what you call the baptism of the Holy Spirit and fire, so that we can be your effective and compelling witnesses to the end of the earth, just like you witnessed for Yahweh!"

Since the disciples stayed put in Jerusalem, they must have all come into agreement that they needed to wait to be clothed with power from on high, **BEFORE** they moved forward in being Jesus's witnesses! And so they did...

"When the day of Pentecost had come, they were all in one place. And suddenly a sound came from heaven like the rush of a mighty wind, and it filled all the house where they were sitting. And there appeared to them **TONGUES AS OF FIRE**, distributing and resting on each one of them. And they were all **FILLED WITH THE HOLY SPIRIT** and began to speak in other tongues, as the Spirit gave them utterance" (Acts 2:1-4).

Remember Jesus said he would baptize with the **HOLY SPIRIT and with FIRE**. The tongues of fire seen resting upon the disciples was proof of what took place on that day, so there would be no doubt of what just happened.

Peter described to the crowds what they were witnessing when the disciples all began speaking in other tongues the **MIGHTY WORKS OF GOD**. "This Jesus God raised up, and of that we all are witnesses. Being therefore exalted at the right hand of God, and having received from the Father the **PROMISE OF THE HOLY SPIRIT**, he (Jesus) **HAS POURED OUT** this which you see and hear" (Acts 2:32-33).

On the day of Pentecost, Jesus fulfilled his promise to his disciples, by clothing them with the same power of the Holy Spirit that he himself had received on the day of his baptism. "How God anointed Jesus of Nazareth with the **HOLY SPIRIT and with POWER**; how he went about doing good and healing all that were oppressed by the devil, for God was with him" (Acts 10:38).

# What a GREAT day at church!

It wasn't until the disciples were baptized by Jesus with the baptism of the Holy Spirit through tongues of fire falling down upon them from heaven that the disciples received the power to become Jesus's bold witnesses to the ends of the earth.

It wasn't until Pentecost that they were able to preach the Gospel boldly, to heal the sick, and to cast out demons in Jesus's name.

Because the disciples began speaking the Good News of Jesus Christ in both word and in power after the fire fell from heaven, scripture records that over 3000 souls were baptized on the day of Pentecost, becoming children of God. Now don't miss this...

> **"** over 3,000 souls were baptized on the day of Pentecost

3000 people became followers of Jesus Christ on the day of Pentecost, because 3000 people **BELIEVED** the testimonies the disciples **SPOKE** about Jesus, disciples who allowed Jesus to baptize them with the Holy Spirit and Fire.

When the fire fell from heaven, and the disciples were baptized with the Holy Spirit, the first thing that happened is they opened their mouths and uttered not their own words, but what they heard their Father saying through the Holy Spirit. The first thing they did is **WITNESS**, by speaking the **MIGHTY WORKS OF GOD** in a language they didn't even understand!

As a result of opening their mouths and letting the Holy Spirit speak through them, 3000 souls were **HARVESTED** for Yahweh's kingdom in just one day. So being baptized with the Holy Spirit is about being a witness in order to bring in a harvest. In fact, God said to me one day, "Being clothed with my power is **ALL ABOUT THE HARVEST!**"

The disciples were compelling and effective witnesses for Jesus Christ, because they allowed Jesus to baptize them with his power to be his witnesses. Because the disciples **DID NOT LIMIT** Jesus in his desire to baptize them with the **FULLNESS** of the Holy Spirit for his kingdom purposes, **3000** people became followers of Jesus Christ in one day!

So my question is this, "Why aren't we seeing the same results as the first church did, in bringing people to Christ? The Good News of Jesus Christ has not changed. The Gospel message is the same as it was yesterday. So what is missing?"

Unfortunately, what has changed is that a very large majority of believers in Jesus Christ have not followed Jesus's instructions and waited for him to baptize them with his power to be his witnesses to the ends of the earth. And because believers are trying to be Jesus's witnesses using their own **HUMAN POWER**, they are having limited results! Before the disciples received the baptism of the Holy Spirit, they were not bold speakers, they were not able to heal the sick, and they could not cast out demons. However, after receiving the baptism of the Holy Spirit, they had these incredible gifts.

**NOW THAT'S HEAVENLY POWER!!!**

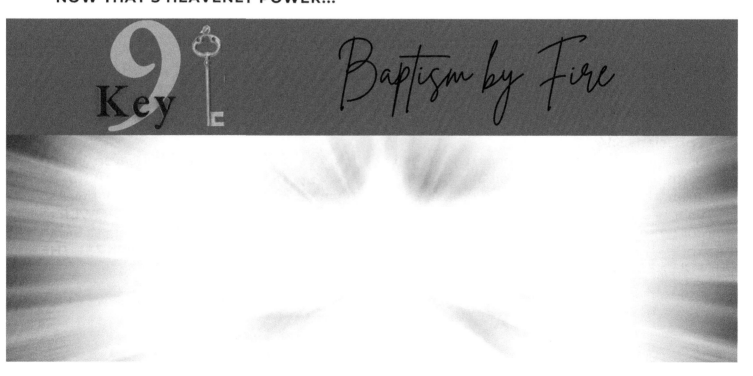

Key 9    Baptism by Fire

Because the disciples allowed the Holy Spirit to speak through their mouths, and miracles, signs and wonders followed them wherever they went, people believed what the disciples spoke about Jesus and became followers of Jesus Christ themselves.

So my question to every believer is this, "After the day of your salvation took place, the day the Holy Spirit came to dwell within you, did you then **WAIT** to receive the **PROMISE of the FATHER**? Did you wait to be baptized with the Holy Spirit and Fire as was promised to Jesus's disciples?"

Jesus needed his first disciples to be **FULLY EQUIPPED**!

Jesus needs **YOU** to be **FULLY EQUIPPED**!

So, if you haven't waited for Jesus to baptize you with the Holy Spirit and Fire, you need to come into **ONE ACCORD** with Jesus, come into **UNION** with Jesus, and pray for his dreams and desires for you to come to fruition, with absolutely **NO LIMITATIONS!**

If you don't know if you have received the baptism of the Holy Spirit and Fire, which is a separate event from your water baptism, then I would imagine you haven't. From my own experience, there was a definite before and after.

So please... I urgently plead with every believer today, who reads these words, to come into complete union with Jesus Christ by asking him to the baptize you with the Holy Spirit and Fire. As Yahweh's children, we need to stop grieving his heart on this important matter, and receive all that Jesus has for us.

Please don't wait...Jesus needs a multitude of **POWERFUL LABORERS** to bring in **HIS HARVEST** for such a time as this!!!


**Matthew 5:6**
"**BLESSED** are those who **HUNGER** and **THIRST** for righteousness, for they **SHALL BE FILLED**."

**1 Peter 2:9**
"But you are a chosen race, a royal priesthood, a holy nation, **GOD'S OWN PEOPLE**, that you may **DECLARE** the wonderful deeds of him who called you out of darkness into his marvelous light."

**Ephesians 3:14**
"For this reason I bow my knees before the Father, from whom every family in heaven and on earth is named, that according to the riches of his glory he may grant you to be strengthened with **MIGHT** through his Spirit in the inner man, and that Christ may dwell in your hearts through faith; that you, being rooted and grounded in love, may have **POWER** to comprehend with all the saints what is the breadth and length and height and depth, and to know the love of Christ which surpasses knowledge, that you **MAY BE FILLED with ALL THE FULLNESS OF GOD**."

# Receiving the Baptism of the Holy Spirit:

## 01 BELIEVE

**BELIEVE** that Jesus desires to bless you with the Promise of the Father, called the baptism of the Holy Spirit and Fire.

## 02 PRAY

**PRAY** to receive the baptism of the Holy Spirit in one accord with Jesus's desires, until the day you receive it.

## 03 WAIT

**WAIT** to receive the baptism of the Holy Spirit, just as Jesus instructed his first disciples.

## 04 TELL

**TELL** Jesus, "Let it be to ME according to your WORD!" with no if, and, or but....

## 05 RECEIVE

**RECEIVE** the fullness of Jesus's power when it comes upon you, being careful not to limit him with your own knowledge of what you think you may or may not be receiving.

## 06 ALLOW

**ALLOW** Jesus to use you as his effective and compelling witnesses, because of his power and boldness flowing through you, and through the gifts of the Holy Spirit you are blessed with.

## 07 SHARE

**SHARE** the Gospel of Jesus Christ to the ends of the earth!

**KEY #9 QUESTIONS:**
Before today, have you ever heard of the baptism of the Holy Spirit?

_____

_____

_____

_____

Have you received the baptism of the Holy Spirit? If you haven't, do you desire to receive it?

_____

_____

_____

_____

If you have received the baptism of the Holy Spirit, write down your testimony of that day.

_____

_____

_____

_____

Write your thoughts on how your life has changed since you were baptized with the Holy Spirit.

_____

_____

_____

_____

**PRAYER:** Heavenly Father, thank you for wanting to baptize all of your children with the Holy Spirit, just like your disciples were baptized on the day of Pentecost. I now understand that the baptism of the Holy Spirit is the **MORE** that you **NEED** all of your children to receive, so that we can be Jesus's witness to everyone we meet, to the ends of the earth. I now know that you need me to be baptized with the Holy Spirit so that I can join you in bringing in the final harvest of souls into your Kingdom, by walking in Jesus's power and authority. Father, please baptize me now with your precious Holy Spirit, so I too can walk with your miracles, signs and wonders following me for the rest of my days. I pray all of these things in Jesus's wonderful name. Amen!

# Father, What else do you want me to know, understand, or believe?

# Key #10 Discover your Gifts of the Holy Spirit

On November 4, 2010, I caught a cold. After about five days, my cold went away except for a residual cough. I didn't really think much about it, until about week twelve. I decided to finally see a doctor, or should I say doctors. After visiting many specialists and enduring many tests, I still had no answer to why I was coughing. It was during this time that I found myself standing in front of the Christian Inspiration aisle at a bookstore. I needed something to read, so I asked Yahweh, "What do you want me to read?" Out of the corner of my eye I caught a glimpse of a book on healing, titled, "**POWER TO HEAL**," by Joan Hunter. I thought maybe it would help me with my cough. So, I bought the book.

As I began to read, I quickly realized that the author of the book had received the **GIFT OF HEALING** from the Holy Spirit. When she lays her hands on people, they are healed. Her parents had this gift as well. So I continued reading the book, and by the time I was finished, I was jealous. I wasn't even thinking about my cough anymore or how I could receive my own healing; instead, I was thinking about how jealous I was of this woman's gift. Not that I wanted the gift of healing, but I wanted my own gift from the Holy Spirit. Of course, Yahweh knew this would be the case. Many times during my walk with him he used my jealousy in order to push me further down the path he has planned for me.

On the night I finished the book, I did something I had never done before. I lifted my hands into the air towards heaven and boldly said, **"GOD, I WANT EVERYTHING THE HOLY SPIRIT HAS TO OFFER ME! DON'T HOLD BACK!"** It was a request I had never made before. Because Yahweh had brought me to a place of peace, I could finally see all that he had done for me through the years. Therefore, I was ready to do whatever he called me to do for his kingdom. On that night, I asked my Lord and Savior to send me everything the Holy Spirit had to offer me. I had no agenda in mind when I made that request; I just knew I wanted it all! For the first time ever, I truly surrendered my entire life to God's will.

On that night, it was as if I were saying, "**HERE I AM LORD, SEND ME**." From that day forward **EVERYTHING CHANGED**. Quickly, I came to find out that the Holy Spirit has a lot to offer. What I discovered about a year later was the night I asked for everything is the night when Jesus baptized me with the Holy Spirit and with Fire. What immediately changed was my ability to hear Yahweh's majestic voice. Suddenly, I was encountering his voice daily. Because I made myself completely available to work for his kingdom, he opened up a whole new way of communication, which is available to everyone who sacrifices himself wholly to furthering Yahweh's kingdom.

www.JUDYJACOBSONMINISTRIES.com

# Key 10

## Gifts from the Holy Spirit

Over the next several years, Yahweh also gave me an abundance of gifts from the Holy Spirit. He asked me to write a book about his divine name, start a prophetic prayer ministry, lay hands on the sick, and teach Christians how to hear his majestic voice. Through these spiritual gifts, I have played my part in miracles, signs, and wonders taking place in other people's lives, in Jesus's mighty name. Since working for Yahweh's kingdom, my mind has been completely transformed and renewed, I am able to interpret Yahweh's Word with clarity, and I have a boldness to witness for Yahweh and Jesus to everyone I meet.

I desire for every believer in Jesus Christ to experience their own **ENCOUNTERS with THE GREAT I AM** and to receive their own gifts from the Holy Spirit. Remember, the gifts of the Holy Spirit are given for the purpose of furthering Yahweh's kingdom on earth as it is in heaven.

Jesus said, "And these signs will accompany those who believe: **IN MY NAME** they will **CAST OUT DEMONS**; they will speak in new tongues; ... they will **LAY THEIR HANDS ON THE SICK**, and they will recover." (Mark 16:17-18)

Jesus also said, "Truly, truly, I say to you, he who believes in me will also do the works that I do; and **GREATER WORKS** than these will he do, because I go to the Father." (John 14:12)

"And preach as you go, saying, 'The kingdom of heaven is at hand. **HEAL THE SICK, RAISE THE DEAD, CLEANSE THE LEPERS, CAST OUT DEMONS**. You received without paying, give without pay.'" (Matthew 10:7-8)

So desire the gifts of the Holy Spirit, so you too can start working for God's kingdom in your daily life.

# Spiritual Gifts

**1 Corinthians 12:1-11**

Now concerning spiritual gifts, brethren, I do not want you to be uninformed. You know that when you were heathen, you were led astray to dumb idols, however you may have been moved. Therefore I want you to understand that no one speaking by the Spirit of God ever says "Jesus be cursed!" and no one can say "Jesus is Lord" except by the Holy Spirit. Now there are varieties of **GIFTS**, but the same Spirit; and there are varieties of **SERVICE** but the same Lord; and there are varieties of **WORKING**, but it is the same God who inspires them all in every one. To each is given the **MANIFESTATION OF THE SPIRIT** for the common good. To one is given through the Spirit the **UTTERANCE OF WISDOM**, and to another the **UTTERANCE OF KNOWLEDGE** according to the same Spirit, to another **FAITH** by the same Spirit, to another **GIFTS OF HEALING** by the one Spirit, to another the **WORKING OF MIRACLES**, to another **PROPHECY**, to another the ability to **DISTINGUISH BETWEEN SPIRITS**, to another various kinds of **TONGUES**, to another the **INTERPRETATION OF TONGUES**. All these are inspired by one and the same Spirit, who apportions to each one individually as he wills."

**1 Corinthians 14:1**
*"Make love your aim, and **EARNESTLY DESIRE** the spiritual gifts, especially that you may **PROPHESY**."*

**Ephesians 4:1-8,11-16**

"I therefore, a prisoner for the Lord, beg you to lead a life worthy of the calling to which you have been called, with all lowliness and meekness, with patience, forbearing one another in love, eager to maintain the unity of the Spirit in the bond of peace. There is one body and one Spirit, just as you were called to the one hope that belongs to your call, one Lord, one faith, one baptism, one God and Father of us all, who is above all and through all and in all. But grace was given to each of us according to the measure of Christ's gift. Therefore it is said, "When he ascended on high he led a host of captives, and **HE GAVE GIFTS TO MEN** ... And his gifts were that some should be **APOSTLES**, some **PROPHETS**, some **EVANGELISTS**, some **PASTORS** and **TEACHERS**, to equip the saints for the work of ministry, for building up the body of Christ, until we all attain to the unity of the faith and of the knowledge of the Son of God, to mature manhood, to the measure of the stature of the fulness of Christ; so that we may no longer be children, tossed to and fro and carried about with every wind of doctrine, by the cunning of men, by their craftiness in deceitful wiles. Rather, speaking the truth in love, we are to grow up in every way into him who is the head, into Christ, from whom the whole body, joined and knit together by every joint with which it is supplied, when each part is working properly, makes bodily growth and upbuilds itself in love."

**KEY #10 QUESTIONS:**
Father, what spiritual gifts have you currently blessed me with?

_____

_____

_____

_____

Father, am I currently utilizing the gifts the Holy Spirit has given me?

_____

_____

_____

_____

Father, in what situations would you like me to utilize the gifts you have given me?

_____

_____

_____

_____

_____

Father, what spiritual gifts do you earnestly want me to desire, knowing that you want to give me the desires of my heart (Psalm 37:4)?

_____

_____

_____

_____

_____

**PRAYER:** Heavenly Father, thank you for sending your Holy Spirit, in Jesus's name, to reside within me so that I can hear and see your majestic voice through the countless ways in which you speak. I ask for you to empower me, with the gifts the Holy Spirit has selected specifically for me. I earnestly desire the spiritual gifts, especially to prophesy, so that I too can help build up and encourage the body of Christ through your personal messages. Teach me how to wisely and humbly utilize the precious gifts you have given me. For I desire to do the Greater Works that Jesus prophesied your disciples would do, so as to further your Kingdom on earth. I thank you Father, Son, and Holy Spirit for richly blessing me with your goodness. I pray all of these things in Jesus's priceless name. Amen!

# Father, What else do you want me to know, understand, or believe?

# Key #11 Utilize the Gift of Speaking in Tongues

Speaking in tongues is a gift of the Holy Spirit that comes with very **POWERFUL BENEFITS** that Yahweh wants to lovingly give all of his children through the Baptism of the Holy Spirit. It is a mysterious heavenly language spoken between Yahweh's Holy Spirit within you, and Yahweh himself.

Because speaking in tongues is a mystery that cannot be truly understood and explained, we have to take Paul's words as truth, "For one who speaks in a tongue **SPEAKS NOT TO MEN BUT TO GOD**; for no one understands him, but he **UTTERS MYSTERIES IN THE SPIRIT**...He who speaks in a tongue **EDIFIES HIMSELF**..." ( 1 Corinthians 14:2,4)

According to Yahweh, speaking in tongues will strengthen and empower you and can be used to fight and defeat the enemy in your life. It is a language that is pleasing to him, and music to his ears. So even though speaking in tongues may seem weird and crazy, we have to remember whom the gift comes from. Yahweh wouldn't give us a gift from heaven that wasn't beneficial to us. We need to trust our Heavenly Father that he has our best interest at heart.

It is actually very freeing to know when you run out of words in your prayer time that you can start speaking in tongues, at which point the Holy Spirit that dwells inside of you will take over your conversation with Yahweh, in order to achieve the best results in any circumstance.

In reference to speaking in tongues, Yahweh told me one day, "**MY WORDS ARE BETTER THAN YOURS.**" His message made me laugh out loud, because he is right. So I make sure to speak in Yahweh's **HEAVENLY LANGUAGE** every time I meet with him, so that heaven can be brought to earth in a greater measure for me and my family, and every person, situation, or circumstance that comes my way.

The depth of Yahweh's message, about how his words are better than mine, was made clear to me on the day that Jesus delivered a man from demonic oppression through my hands, and two other women. Yahweh asked us to pray for a man who, if diagnosed, would have been labeled a schizophrenic, as he heard demonic voices in his head. God told us that if we prayed for him, a miracle would occur and he would be freed of all that ailed him. So we did as Yahweh instructed, even though we were **VERY UNQUALIFIED** for the task.

On the day of this prayer session, I came spiritually armed with what Yahweh had given me the day before: a dream, words of knowledge, and the gift of speaking in tongues. That's it. That's all I was given by Yahweh. It didn't seem like enough, and yet Yahweh knew that was all I would need.

      WWW.JUDYJACOBSONMINISTRIES.com

To make a long story short, Jesus completely delivered this man of 13 demons, after 5 **hours** of prayer, through our obedience of using the tools Yahweh gave us, and our faith that with Yahweh **ALL THINGS ARE POSSIBLE.**

Even though we spoke a lot of English words on that night, I wholeheartedly believe this man was delivered from demonic oppression, because we **ALLOWED** Yahweh's Holy Spirit to speak his powerful words into this man's situation, through our mouths. We do not know what Yahweh's Holy Spirit spoke into this man's ears or into the atmosphere on this night. What we do know is **YAHWEH'S WORDS** cast out all of this man's demons and sent them fleeing, never to harm him again.

What an amazing testimony of utilizing Yahweh's powerful gift of speaking in tongues!

And, if that story doesn't convince you of the power of speaking in tongues, I also have two other stories of times when Yahweh personally commanded me to speak in tongues. The first time he did this, he woke me in the night and simply told me to pray in tongues for my son. I had no idea why. However, I obeyed by praying in tongues for the next 90 minutes, without knowing what the Holy Spirit was praying through me. Am I forever thankful that I did! Because of my obedience, I found out the next day that my son's life was spared from death that night. Thank you Jesus!

The second time Yahweh commanded me to speak in tongues, with no explanation on why, my family's home was spared from catching on fire, from our neighbor's house that was completely engulfed in flames. Both of these situations, which would have been extremely life altering, did not come to fruition, because I utilized the Holy Spirit's very powerful gift of speaking in tongues upon Yahweh's command.

So **EARNESTLY DESIRE** the gift of speaking in tongues, receive it, and then pray in tongues daily. You will never regret that you did!

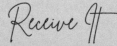

**1 Corinthians 14:39**
"So, my brethren, earnestly desire to prophesy, and **DO NOT FORBID SPEAKING IN TONGUES**;"

**Acts 2:4**
And they were all filled with the Holy Spirit and began to **SPEAK IN OTHER TONGUES** as the Spirit gave them utterance.

**Acts 19:6**
And when Paul had laid his hands on them, the Holy Spirit came on them, and they **SPOKE WITH TONGUES** and prophesied.

**1 Corinthians 14:2,4**
For one who speaks in a tongue **SPEAKS NOT TO MEN BUT TO GOD**; for no one understands him, but he **UTTERS MYSTERIES IN THE SPIRIT**...He who speaks in a tongue **EDIFIES HIMSELF**...

**KEY #11 QUESTIONS:**
Have you received the gift of speaking in tongues? If your answer is yes, then journal your experience.

_____
_____
_____
_____

If you have not, what are your thoughts about speaking in tongues?

_____
_____
_____

If you are hesitant to receive this gift, ask your heavenly Father, "Why am I hesitant to receive this gift from you?"

_____
_____
_____
_____

Father, what are the benefits of me speaking in tongues?

_____
_____
_____
_____

For more information on the benefit of speaking in tongues, I highly recommend the book titled, "**Speaking in Tongues: Your Secret Weapon**," by Todd Smith.

**PRAYER:** Heavenly Father, thank you for you precious gift of speaking in tongues. I now understand the many benefits of this mysterious gift that you desire to give all of your children. I trust you Father that you have my best interests at heart, and that is why you desire for me to have, and to use, this powerful weapon daily. For I now understand that by allowing your Holy Spirit to speak through my lips, with your heavenly language, that you are blessing me in ways that I could only imagine. Therefore, Holy Spirit, I give you access to my mouth. I ask you to speak the will of Yahweh through my lips, so I can bring heaven to earth in a greater measure. Please bless me with the gift of speaking in tongues from this day forward. It is in Jesus's passionate name that I pray. Amen!

# Father, What else do you want me to know, understand, or believe?

_____
_____
_____
_____
_____
_____
_____
_____
_____
_____
_____
_____
_____
_____
_____
_____
_____
_____
_____
_____
_____
_____
_____
_____
_____
_____

# Key #12 Engage with Yahweh's Angels

One day a man approached my car in a grocery store parking lot, and then knocked on my window. When I rolled down my window he said, "**DID YOU KNOW THAT TOMORROW IS THE FIRST DAY OF THE REST OF YOUR LIFE?**", and then he left. I had never seen this man before and I haven't seen him since. It was definitely a strange encounter I will never forget. I pondered his words for days, because they were said with such conviction, and yet he didn't hang around for my reply.

I now know without a doubt this man was one of Yahweh's angels sent in human form from heaven, in order to give me this personal message!

I know this, because several years later Yahweh continued his message about tomorrow being the first day of the rest of your life, when he said to me one night, "**TOMORROW IS THE DAY!**" He said it audibly, as if he was standing right next to me. Since Yahweh had never spoken audibly to me before, he had my complete attention. I replied to Yahweh, "**TOMORROW IS THE DAY FOR WHAT?**"

The next day Yahweh continued his message by saying, "**TODAY IS THE DAY!**" Again, I replied, "**TODAY IS THE DAY FOR WHAT?**" I was confused. What did Yahweh want me to know about today? Obviously, it was very important to him, as he had chosen to speak to me audibly. So, I did what I knew to do; I went to BibleGateway and looked up every verse that had the word "today" in it. Wow...the very first verse read:

"**TODAY, WHEN YOU HEAR MY VOICE, DO NOT HARDEN YOUR HEART.**" (Hebrew 3:7-8)

When I read this verse, the angel's message to me about tomorrow being the first day of the rest of my life, came back to my mind, and I knew exactly what Yahweh wanted me to know. For when we start **LISTENING** to and **OBEYING** Yahweh's voice, our life will begin to be completely transformed with his truth and wisdom, instead of Satan's worldly lies. Therefore, **TOMORROW** could truly become the **FIRST DAY** of the rest of your life, when you start living abundantly being guided by Yahweh and Jesus's majestic voice!

What an amazing message I received from Yahweh on that day. And to think it all began with him sending one of his heavenly angels, in order to **PREPARE THE WAY** for me to receive his incredible word!

Through this encounter I was awakened to the fact that Yahweh's angels are real, and are sent out daily by Yahweh to accomplish his kingdom purposes. Since that day I have had numerous encounters with Yahweh's angels. And although I have rarely seen them, I have definitely benefitted from their work in my life, as with each encounter I received another powerful message from Yahweh.

So, what else do we know about Yahweh's angels?

We actually know quite a bit about them, considering there are over **280** verses in the Bible concerning angels and their purpose, with **72** verses about angels in the book of Revelation alone. We see throughout the Old and New Testament story after story of biblical characters interacting with angels in dreams, visions and in human form. From the beginning of times, angels have been sent by Yahweh to speak instructions and warnings, and to announce the birth of Jesus. They were sent to minister, to guard, to awaken, to prepare the way, to block the way, to fight, to save from destruction, and to redirect his children. From these stories we know that there are awakening angels, revelatory angels, scribe angels, healing angels, and deliverance angels. There are protective angels, guardian angels, prosperity angels, and destroying angels. In a nutshell, from reading all of the Bible verses, it becomes apparent that whatever work Yahweh needs to have done on earth for his children, by **HIS COMMAND**, he will send one or more of his angels in order to help **CARRY OUT HIS WILL**.

One day Yahweh said to me: "**ANGELS ARE EMPLOYED BY ME. THEY ARE AT YOUR SERVICE, SO USE THEM**." I asked Yahweh, "**HOW DO I USE YOUR ANGELS**?" He replied, "**ASK ME**."

Hebrews 1:14 says, "Are they (angels) not all **MINISTERING SPIRITS SENT FORTH TO SERVE**, for the sake of those who are to obtain salvation?" Therefore, we can ask Yahweh to send his mighty angels to protect and guard our family and children, our homes, property, and vehicles. We can ask Yahweh to send his angels ahead of us, wherever we go, in order to prepare our way for success, or to help fight our battles. We can ask Yahweh to send his mighty angels to change the atmosphere in our work places, or to awaken people to him. If the Holy Spirit places it on you to ask Yahweh to send his angels somewhere, or to do something, then ask him. Scripture says that angels are ministering spirits sent forth by Yahweh to serve his sons and daughters, so we need to use them in order to help bring heaven to earth!

In addition, Psalm 103:20 says, "Bless Yahweh, O you his angels, you mighty ones **WHO DO HIS WORD**, **HEARKENING to THE VOICE of his WORD**!" What Yahweh has revealed to me is that just as angels hearken to the voice of his Word when **HE SPEAKS**, his angels also hearken to the voice of his sons and daughters when **WE SPEAK** his Word out of their mouths.

What this means is that when we **DECLARE** Yahweh's Word out of our mouths, whether they are Biblical truths or personal promises from Yahweh himself, our angel's ears perk up, and they go to work on our behalf. Remember the word engage means, "to participate or become involved in." Therefore, we engage with Yahweh's kingdom angels by asking Yahweh to send them out where they are needed, and by declaring Yahweh's truth out of our mouths daily.

Unfortunately, what Yahweh has shown me is there are a lot of bored angels standing around doing nothing, because the believer they have been assigned to knows nothing about the role of Yahweh's angels and is therefore not engaging and collaborating with them. So please ask Yahweh to teach you everything there is to know about his mighty angels, so that you too can benefit from their work in your life.

For further reading, I highly recommend a book titled, "**The Divinity Code to Understanding Angels**," by Adam F. Thompson, and Adrian Beale. It will definitely make you aware of the angelic activity going on around you and how you too can co-labor with Yahweh's angels in order to accomplish Yahweh's will on earth, as it is in heaven.

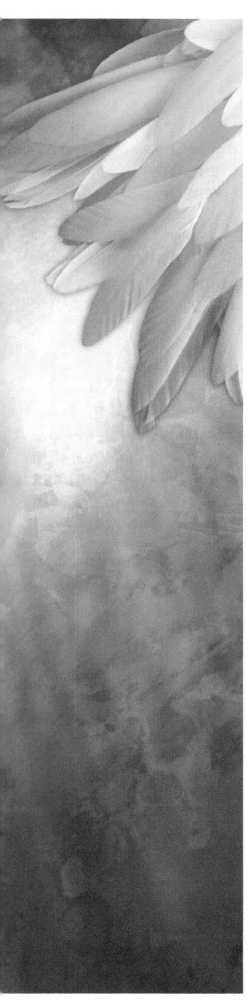

# Key 12 Angels

**Revelation 5:11** (Myriads of worshiping angels)
Then I looked, and I heard around the throne and the living creatures and the elders **THE VOICE OF MANY ANGELS**, numbering myriads of myriads and thousands of thousands, saying with a loud voice, "Worthy is the Lamb who was slain, to receive power and wealth and wisdom and might, and honor and glory and blessing!"

**Matthew 4:11** (Ministering angels)
"Then the devil left him, and behold, angels came and **MINISTERED TO HIM**."

**Luke 1:19** (Angel Delivers Message)
"And the angel answered him, 'I am Gabriel, who stand in the presence of God, and **I WAS SENT TO SPEAK TO YOU, and to bring you this GOOD NEWS.**"

**Revelation 22:16** (Angel Delivers Messages)
"I Jesus have **SENT MY ANGEL** to you with this **TESTIMONY** for the churches. I am the root and the offspring of David, the bright morning star."

**Revelation 19:10** (Angels are not to be worshipped)
Then I fell down at his feet to worship him (an angel), but he said to me, "You must not do that! I am a **FELLOW SERVANT** with you and your brethren who hold the testimony of Jesus. Worship God."

**Psalm 91:11** (Guardian angels)
Because you have made Yahweh your refuge, the Most High your habitation... For he will give his angels **CHARGE OF YOU to GUARD YOU** in all your ways. On their hands they will bear you up, lest you dash your foot against a stone.

**Matthew 18:10** (Guardian angel assigned to everyone)
"See that you do not despise one of these little ones; for I tell you that in heaven **THEIR ANGELS** always behold the face of my Father who is in heaven."

# Angels

**Psalm 34:7** (Delivering angels)
The angel of Yahweh **ENCAMPS** around those who fear him, and **DELIVERS** them.

**Daniel 6:22** (Protective angels)
"My God sent his angel and **SHUT THE LION'S MOUTH**, and they have not hurt me, because I was found blameless before him; and also before you, O king, I have done no wrong."

**2 Kings 6:15-17** (Angel armies)
When the servant of the man of God rose early in the morning and went out, behold, an army with horses and chariots was round about the city. And the servant said, "Alas my master! What shall we do?" He said, "**FEAR NOT**, for those **WHO ARE WITH US** are **MORE** than those who are with them." Then Elisha prayed, and said, "O Yahweh I pray thee, open his eyes that he may see." So Yahweh opened the eyes of the young man, and he saw; and behold the mountain was full of horses and chariots of fire round about Elisha.

**Matthew 26:52-53** (Appealing to God to send his angels) Then Jesus said to him... "Do you think that I cannot **APPEAL TO MY FATHER**, and he will at once send me more than twelve legions (72,000) of angels?"

**Hebrews 13:2** (Angels in human form)
Do not neglect to show hospitality to strangers, for thereby some have **ENTERTAINED ANGELS** unawares.

**Matthew 16:19** (Angels carry out binding and loosing)
"I will give you the keys of the kingdom of heaven, and whatever you **BIND** on earth shall be **BOUND** in heaven, and whatever you **LOOSE** on earth shall be **LOOSED** in heaven."

**KEY #12 QUESTIONS:**
Father, have I ever encountered one of your mighty angels, maybe without even knowing it? If I have, then please bring that memory to my mind now, so that I can journal my experience.

_____

_____

_____

_____

_____

Father, am I currently using your angels by declaring your Word, or are the angels assigned to me bored?

_____

_____

_____

_____

_____

_____

Father, in what current situations do you want me to utilize your angels by declaring your Word?

_____

_____

_____

_____

_____

_____

**PRAYER:** Heavenly Father, I thank you for your army of angels that you readily send out to help your precious children. Please teach me everything I need to know about your angels and their heavenly role of guarding, ministering, and deliver messages to me and my family. I too desire to experience encounters with your angels in dreams, visions, and in the natural world, just like your children did in biblical times. Teach me to engage with your angels by declaring your Word out of my mouth regularly. Open my senses to feel their angelic presence around me, and to see their tangible activity in my life and the life of others. Thank you for giving me your wisdom about your mighty angels. In the divine name of Jesus Christ of Nazareth, I pray all of these things. Amen!

# Father, What else do you want me to know, understand, or believe?

# The Abundant Life

Years ago, I was thinking about the state of the world and how far we have come from the Garden of Eden. As you probably know, life was absolutely perfect for Adam and Eve, until they were deceived into eating from the tree of knowledge of good and evil. For Satan had them believing that if they ate of this tree their eyes would be opened, and they would become like God. Ultimately Adam and Eve made the wrong decision to eat from this tree, by disobeying Yahweh's **ONE** and **ONLY** commandment, and as a result they were kicked out of their oasis, out of Yahweh's Presence.

As I was pondering all that took place in the Garden of Eden, I was saddened to think that the majority of mankind has continued to eat from the tree of knowledge of good and evil ever since. It's not hard to see the mess man has created, across all mountains of society across the world, by playing "god" with all their so-called knowledge throughout the centuries.

While visualizing the mess man has created, I imagined Yahweh having a conversation with Jesus saying, "**YOU KNOW SON... MAYBE THIS WHOLE FREEWILL IDEA WAS A BAD ONE.**"

After chuckling, I told Yahweh, "Lord, I am handing back my freewill to you. It has gotten me into trouble my entire life, and I don't want it anymore. I know that your will for my life is so much better than my own. Therefore, I don't want to play god any longer. Instead, I want **YOUR WILL to be MY WILL**. So please take my freewill. I give you permission to take back your precious gift from me."

Even though I knew this wasn't an option, and that I couldn't just hand back my freewill, I guess I still wanted God to know my heart's desire. For I truly desire for the rest of my life to consist of Yahweh's will, his thoughts, truth, agenda, purpose, dreams and visions for me, instead of my own.

Even though God didn't take back my freewill, what happened next is really cool. God gave me the **HOW TO** of daily giving up my will for his will.

Yahweh first gave me a dream, in which I was teaching a group of believers how to relinquish control of our flesh over to the Holy Spirit within us. I then practiced for about a week what I heard myself teaching others to do in my dream. And finally, at the end of that week, I received confirmation that what I was doing was making a noticeable difference in handing over my freewill to my heavenly Father.

## MY DREAM

I had a dream of gathering some people of all different levels of faith outside on a driveway to discuss how believers in Jesus Christ could keep from "catching" the corona virus. In my dream, I knew the corona virus represented all the worldly physical, emotional, and spiritual "dis-eases and viruses" that currently plague mankind.

Like other dreams I've had recently, it was hard to get the people to be quiet, in order to listen to what I had to say. Right before I think they were finally going to be quiet and still, Ben and Michelle walk by me with food in their hands. One dish looked very green and healthy and freshly made. The other dish looked like processed food, kind of like a round pizza pocket. I later came to realize that the fresh and healthy dish represented food from the tree of life, while the processed dish represented food from the tree of knowledge. In my dream each person had a freewill choice on what they were going to eat.

While I was trying to gather everyone together to listen, several people started asking me random questions about worldly beliefs: horoscopes and new age stuff. I told them, "**ALL OF THAT IS WORLDLY NONSENSE. THIS IS WHAT GOD WANTS YOU TO KNOW**."

I first asked everyone if they had ever felt chill bumps from the Lord, when hearing something that they knew was true. Only about half of the people raised their hands. I continued by explaining to them how what they are feeling, when they felt chill bumps, was actually Yahweh's Spirit within them **WITNESSING** to them the truth of what they had just heard or realized.

That feeling of chill bumps is the Holy Spirit **COMING OUT OF YOUR SPIRIT** and **ENTERING INTO YOUR FLESH**.

I then explained that God had given me instructions on how to defeat the "corona viruses" of this world. God told me we are to **RELINQUISH ALL CONTROL** of our flesh, **OVER TO** his Holy Spirit in Jesus's name that is within us. We are to surrender all of our fleshly desires to the Holy Spirit, because the Holy Spirit within us is **IMMUNE to all DIS-EASE**. Yahweh's Spirit in Jesus's name cannot be spiritually, emotionally, or physically sick. Therefore, we need to give God's Spirit within us **PERMISSION** to reign over our souls (our minds, will, and emotions), and over our physical flesh in order to be healed of all that ails us.

I then woke up from my dream...but my thoughts continued.

**HEALING POWER** for everything that currently ails us, including physical sickness, is already in our Spirits. When you think of it that way, you come to realize that Jesus's healing touch is already extremely close to our soul, and our physical flesh. We therefore need to release God's Spirit into our soul and flesh, in order for healing to take place in our minds, our hearts, our emotions, and in our physical flesh.

**Jesus's will is, AND ALWAYS WILL BE, to heal Yahweh's children**. While Jesus walked this earth, he had a healing, deliverance, and restoration ministry, and he still does. When we come to believe that Jesus died for our sins, we receive salvation, and then the Holy Spirit in Jesus's name comes to dwell within us.

The Greek word for salvation is **SOZO**. The word sozo means to save, heal, deliver, restore, and to make whole. Jesus came to **SOZO** the world. Therefore, the Holy Spirit within us becomes the means by which we are saved, healed, delivered, restored, and made whole.

So, if it's through the Holy Spirit by which all these things take place, we have got to release the Holy Spirit out of our Spirit (the box in which we have the Holy Spirit placed), into our soul and physical flesh!

Wow!!! All of a sudden I understood the **HOW TO** of handing my freewill over, in exchange for Yahweh's will.

There will always be a battle between our flesh and our Spirit. Paul describes this real battle in Scripture many times. Therefore, we need to give Yahweh's Spirit **PERMISSION** to enter into our soul (our mind, our will, our emotions), and our physical flesh, in order to have his way with us, every single day!

I know this sounds crazy, but remember we have been given freewill...

We need to stop limiting the work of Holy Spirit within us with our so-called knowledge and our religious traditions and theology. We need to repent of our false belief systems, when it comes to healing, restoration, and deliverance. We need to repent of every thought or belief within us that may be hindering us from becoming whole. We need to repent of our **FLESHLY CONTROL**.

It is often our mind and beliefs, our flesh, and our pride that is hindering us from being set free. We need to relinquish the 2000 years of religious traditions that are getting in the way of us receiving all that the Holy Spirit has to offer us, and we need to repent of our worldly ways. We need to come into agreement, **INTO COMPLETE UNION**, with Jesus's Spirit within us.

In a nut shell, we need to stop eating from the toxic tree of knowledge, and only eat from the healthy **TREE OF LIFE.**

**MY PERSONAL PRACTICE**

So over the next few days, I practiced what I preached in my dream. Every time I met with the Lord, I began my time with him by relinquishing all control of my mind, my will, my emotions and all of my fleshly thoughts and desires over to the Holy Spirit within me. I also imagined myself releasing God's Holy Spirit within me into my flesh, into every cell of my body, making ever cell completely brand new. I gave God's Holy Spirit permission to have his way with my body and my soul.

After several days of doing this I started **FEELING** God's Holy Spirit entering into my flesh, because I actually **FELT** chill bumps on my skin, while spending quiet time with him. That's when I knew I was on to something. The chill bumps that I felt was my witness that God's Holy Spirit was released out of my spirit, and into my flesh. By the end of the week, all I would have to do is close my eyes, with the intention of relinquishing control of my flesh over to Yahweh's Holy Spirit within me, and immediately I would feel chill bumps on my skin.

I realized that every time I pray I need to release Yahweh's Holy Spirit into my soul and my physical flesh. I also realized that I need to stay in prayer and worship **UNTIL I FEEL** the Holy Spirit in my flesh, as a witness that I have given God's Spirit permission to have his way with me.

I realized that believers often cut Jesus off, by quickly getting up from their prayer time with the Lord, before they have **HEARD** from the Lord, either through his witnessing in their flesh, or by receiving their daily bread through words of knowledge, thoughts, impressions, dreams or visions, etc.

**YAHWEH'S CONFIRMATION**

A few days later, after running on our treadmill, I sat in our sauna. This is a weekly routine for me. My dog Winston has seen me do this many times, and he usually lies down in the basement waiting for me to finish.

The first thing I did, while in the sauna, was relinquish control of my flesh over to Yahweh's Holy Spirit within me. Like always I prayed that Yahweh's Spirit would burn away all fleshly desires, false beliefs, false lies, and false doctrine that were keeping his Spirit from fully reigning in my life. I prayed for only **TRUTH** to be left in my mind and in my heart. I prayed that Yahweh's Spirit would be released into every cell of my body.

After doing this, my son Sam came downstairs and, after finding me in the sauna, he said, **"OH, THERE YOU ARE. WINSTON WAS LOOKING FOR YOU."** And then Sam went back upstairs.

At dinner that night Sam told me what happened that morning. He said that Winston had come to his shut door and started scratching on it. When he opened the door, Winston hurriedly ran down the hall and then downstairs. Sam somehow knew Winston wanted him to follow him. Winston led him right to me in the sauna. Sam indicated that Winston was acting very strange. Sam said, **"I THINK WINSTON THOUGHT YOU WERE DEAD."**

While pondering Sam's statement, I remembered what I was doing in the sauna. I had relinquished all control of my **FLESH to the HOLY SPIRIT** and asked God's Spirit within me to have its way with my soul and my flesh. I asked Yahweh's Spirit within me to **BURN AWAY** all fleshly desires, and thoughts, so that I would walk completely by his Spirit within me.

What I strongly believe is that my dog sensed something was going on. He felt something was different with me. He alerted Sam to what was going on. Sam said, **"I THINK WINSTON THOUGHT YOU WERE DEAD." WOW!!!**

I believe that by relinquishing all control of my flesh to my Spirit, it actually accomplished something in the physical realm that seemed very real to Winston. My dog believed that my **FLESH was DEAD**. It reminded me of stories of when dogs alert people when someone in their family is about to have a seizure or a heart attack. I knew Yahweh had just confirmed all that I was doing.

Relinquishing all control of your flesh to Yahweh's Spirit actually accomplishes more that you could ever imagine. If done daily, it will make a huge impact in your life, because you will start walking in Yahweh's Spirit, being **SPIRIT-LED**, instead of being led by your flesh.

## Abundant Life

I now believe that Yahweh gives us freewill with the hope that we will come to the conclusion one day that we don't want our freewill any longer, thereby desiring his will for our lives. When we come to this conviction, it actually becomes the catalyst in bringing **HEAVEN TO EARTH** in our own lives and in the lives of those around us. For it is when we sacrifice our own flesh, and die to ourselves, that Yahweh's Spirit begins to **REIGN** unhindered, resulting in the **ABUNDANT LIFE!**

**Matthew 6:9-10**
"Our Father, who art in heaven, hallowed by thy name. **THY KINGDOM COME, THY WILL BE DONE**, on earth as it is in heaven."

**Luke 9:23**
And he said to all, "If any man would come after me, let him **DENY HIMSELF** and take up his cross **DAILY** and **FOLLOW ME**."

**John 17:22-23**
"The glory which thou hast given me I have given to them, that they **MAY BE ONE** even as we are one, I in them and thou in me, that they may **BECOME PERFECTLY ONE**, so that the world may know that thou hast sent me and hast loved them even as thou hast loved me."

**2 Corinthians 3:17-18**
"Now the Lord is the Spirit, and where the Spirit of the Lord is, there is freedom. And we all, with unveiled face, beholding the glory of the Lord, are being **CHANGED INTO HIS LIKENESS FROM ONE DEGREE OF GLORY TO ANOTHER**; for this comes from the Lord who is the Spirit."

**Galatians 2:20**
"I have been crucified with Christ; **IT IS NO LONGER I WHO LIVE, BUT CHRIST WHO LIVES IN ME**; and the life I now live in the flesh **I LIVE BY FAITH IN THE SON OF GOD**, who loved me and gave himself for me."

# Father, Do you have any final thoughts that you want me to know?

_____

_____

_____

_____

_____

_____

_____

_____

_____

_____

_____

_____

_____

_____

_____

_____

_____

_____

_____

_____

_____

_____

# Thank You

May Yahweh, your Heavenly Father, bless you and keep you!
May Yahweh make his face to shine upon you and be gracious to you!
May Yahweh lift up his countenance upon you and give you peace!
Numbers 6:22-27

## You can order my book on Amazon.
## "Encountering the Great I AM:
## with HIS NAME comes EVERYTHING"

Made in the USA
Columbia, SC
30 August 2024

40873686R00057